MOTHER SAINT MARY

A living flame today

New Edition

First Publication 1878 by
Burns and Oates, Portman Street
And Paternoster Row, London
Original Title: THE LIFE OF HENRIETTE D'OSSEVILLE
(in religion, Mother St. Mary)
Foundress of the Institute of the Faithful Virgin
Arranged and Edited by John George Macleod,*of the Society of Jesus*

New Edition 2012
by Virgo Fidelis Publications
Title: MOTHER SAINT MARY
A living flame today

This book is dedicated to all the Sisters of the Congregation of
Our Lady of Fidelity who have gone before us and
to the cause of the Canonisation of
Mother Saint Mary

Foreword

This book is dedicated to all the Sisters in the Congregation of Our Lady of Fidelity.

We express our gratitude to
Reverend Mother
Heidi Koller, the Superior General of
The Congregation of Our Lady of Fidelity

Our sincere thanks go to all the Sisters at Norwood for their ideas and enthusiasm and for the many hours spent typing up this book. We especially thank Sister Rosalia who gave up a great deal of her time to edit the book, set the plates, choose the photographs and design the cover. Our heartfelt thanks to Lawrence Farrugia who proof read the entire text and encouraged us every step of the way. We also thank Groundwork Marketing for enabling us to print this book.

'A Living Flame Today' was first published in 1878. We now publish this edition in the hope that many today would be inspired by the life of Mother Saint Mary and that it may play a small part in the cause for her Canonisation.

For myself, this is the realisation of a dream that our Congregation may become better known and that many may answer God's Call to follow Him in the Religious Life in the Congregation of Our Lady of Fidelity.

Sister Bernadette
25th March, 2012

PREFACE

The following life of the Foundress of the Congregation of the Faithful Virgin has been compiled, as its perusal will show, from the first archives of the new Institute, and from letters, chiefly of spiritual direction, addressed to the members of her own community. Although the history of Mother St. Mary and of the work which she achieved does not claim any very marked characteristic of novelty or exciting incident, it cannot fail to be of general interest as describing the career of one raised up by God for the especial work of educating and taking charge of Catholic orphans, than whom there is no class more exposed to danger, particularly in a Protestant country. The Sisters of the Congregation of the Faithful Virgin received the warmest possible welcome on their arrival at Norwood both from Cardinal Wiseman and Bishop Grant, they have been held in the highest esteem by the whole Catholic body in England, and their Foundress must have possessed many sincere personal friends who will be most glad to become, through these pages, further acquainted with the earlier incidents of her life.

The hand of God stamped in deep, sharp lines on her whole course those characteristics by which He invariably accredits to us the founder of a new work. He spared her none of the obstacles, delays, and bitter disappointments which often seem to render almost hopeless the success of an undertaking designed by Him to receive His especial blessing. The opposition which Mother St. Mary had to encounter for a long period was of a very peculiar nature, and singularly harassing and perplexing. But she persevered through all by reason of the deep faith and humility, and the rare confidence in God and conformity to His will, with which her soul was imbued. Her generosity of self-oblation was equalled by her generosity of self-sacrifice, and her disinterestedness may be pronounced truly heroic.

The solid virtue of the infant Congregation was tested in two opposite ways. It had been scarcely formed when Divine Providence called it to a most arduous work, not its own, the attendance on the sick during a terrible visitation of cholera. It was but a little older when it was summoned to the still more trying work of tending for a time the wounded soldiers in the Crimea. This appears a strange training for the special charge of protecting and educating orphans of the poorer class; and, had it not been for the firm and watchful rule of the holy Foundress, directed with a pure and single intention to the one great object of her life, her foundation might have been easily drawn aside from the vocation which had called it into existence. She had the happiness to see that all helped to purify and develope more rapidly the religious tone of her Institute.

The only other point to which the attention of the reader need be drawn is the very marked and careful preparation of Mother St. Mary for her future sphere of usefulness in the Church. Towards this her delicacy of health, her charge of children while still young herself, her easy success and deep interest in winning their affections, and the sacredness of such a vocation in her eyes, are all points to be noticed. The fruit of this preparation may be traced in the fact that the Orphanage at Norwood already contains three hundred and thirty children, and that the work of the nuns of the Faithful Virgin in aiding and directing them by no means ends when the orphans cease to be the inmates of the Covent.

May so great a work find ample support, may it go on and prosper under the blessing of God, the protection of the 'Faithful Virgin', and the favour of the Vicar of Christ!

J. G. McL.

London, Feast of the Assumption, 1878.

Chapter I

Parentage, birth, and childhood of Henriette.

HENRIETTE LE FORESTIER D'OSSEVILLE belonged to a family of the ancient nobility of Normandy, and her father, Count Theodose d'Osseville, was distinguished by his attachment to his legitimate sovereign. His fidelity shone forth conspicuously in the hour of trial, and he sacrificed his fortune in the good cause. He took for his device that of the French knights of old, 'Rather to die than dishonour my name.' During the Great Revolution he married, while still very young, Mademoiselle Anne Renée de Valori, a lady as distinguished as himself for rank and virtue. Their union was blessed by a priest in a poor room. The bride was rather older than her husband, and was endowed with great prudence and gentleness. M. d'Osseville was a very young man, and fond of pleasure. His nobleminded wife determined not to see his errors, but to lay herself out in every way to gain his affections, to meet his wishes, and to make his home attractive to him. Their loss of fortune obliged them to live in a very quiet manner at Mesnil Varin during the summer, and at Rouen during the winter months. It was here that the subject of our biography was born, April 19, 1803. She was one of five children. Of these one daughter died in the flower of her age, the other became Countess de Jumilhac. The two sons both died young. The child of whom we are speaking was baptised the day following her birth at the Abbey of St. Ouen, the only church which had been restored to Catholic worship since the disastrous events of 1793, and received the name of Henriette. A few days after this she nearly met with her death. Whilst the servants were occupied with her mother, her little sister Cecilia, hearing the baby cry, thought it was hungry, and running to it, stuffed its mouth with some of the soft bread-crumbs given her for her own breakfast. She then hastened back to assure her mother she might be quite happy now, for baby would not cry any more, as she had given her plenty to eat. The infant very narrowly escaped being choked to death.

Henriette was brought up at home, her winning gentleness, gaiety, and intelligence making her , at four or five years of age, the plaything of all the household. Her great exactness in saying her daily prayers proved the piety of her heart. The delicacy of her conscience made her afraid even of the appearance of evil, so that her religious children have always felt assured that their beloved Mother had never soiled her baptismal robe. A great love of the poor, early inculcated by her mother, formed one of her distinctive characteristics. She used to relate to her religious children that meeting one day a poor little bare-footed girl, the idea that in this child she saw her Lord struck her with so much force that she felt a desire to bestow a more than ordinary alms. She thought she would take off her own red shoes, which she was wearing for the first time, give them to the little girl, and return barefoot to the house. But the fear of making her mother angry, together with a little human respect, produced a long internal contest, and she allowed the child to go away. She returned sadly to her parents, but never forgot the circumstance, or forgave herself for it. On another occasion she was more faithful to the inspiration of grace. Her mother having given her a little money to spend at a fair, she determined to lay it out in buying preserved plums, which she had only tasted on rare occasions. Just as she was going to purchase them she met a very poor man, and immediately bestowed more than half her treasure upon him. Another time, when walking with her nurse in Rouen, she gave the contents of her purse to a poor wretched-looking woman, whose piteous tale affected her much. Her mother, finding her purse thus completely emptied, was obliged to remind her how slender their own means were.

In her goodness of heart she readily pardoned any wrong inflicted on her; and at home she behaved most gently towards every one who had charge over her. Though her nurse sometimes treated her harshly, yet she never made any complaints to her mother. On one occasion, when accused of having told a lie, the little Henriette merely denied it, but showed no further displeasure, although the woman refused to believe her assertion. She often begged her daughters in religion never to accuse children of falsehood when they asseverate that they have told the truth, unless, indeed, there is clear and abundant proof to the contrary. She would even add that it was better to be sometimes deceived than to run the risk of wounding the heart of a child by false accusation.

Henriette's health had from the beginning given the greatest uneasiness to her parents. As she grew up the weakness of her constitution occasioned a curvature of the spine, and this deformity caused her great suffering all her life, and made her the object of her mother's tenderest solicitude. Madame Dorcher, her godmother, who was childless, being possessed of a large fortune, requested permission to adopt, and make the little child her heiress. But the Countess having reason to fear that her daughter might not receive a good Christian education, declined the seemingly advantageous offer. We shall see how she was recompensed by God for this sacrifice of worldly considerations. Madame d'Osseville brought up her children in habits of the strictest economy, and accustomed them to plain fare, and to the self-denial of not refusing anything that was set before them. When Henriette went to spend a month with one of her aunts, the latter observing that she seemed to relish a dish of spinach offered her at table, was careful to have some served almost every day during her visit. Great, however, was the aunt's surprise and admiration at her ready mortification of her taste, when she learned that this vegetable was particularly distasteful to her.

When nine years old Henriette was present at her elder sister's first Communion. So great was the impression produced on her mind, that from that moment she felt an earnest desire to partake of the same happiness. Her good mother and her confessor, seeing her wish, named Corpus Christi of the year 1815 as the time when she was to receive her first Communion. This, however, seemed to her far too long to wait, and she daily prayed to God that she might receive Him on Easter Tuesday of the same year, having a particular reason for choosing that day. Although the first five weeks of Lent had passed away, and no fresh arrangement had been made, yet her hope was not shaken, for she had confided her trouble and her ardent longing to God, and felt sure she could not be disappointed. It so happened that God made use of public events to procure for His little servant the object of her petition. The unexpected return of Napoleon Buonaparte to France alarmed the venerable priest her confessor, and made him fear lest they might be entering on another Revolution as terrible as the first, in which Catholic worship had been abolished. He therefore proposed to the Countess d'Osseville that her child's first Communion should be fixed for Easter Tuesday, adding that, as he knew her spiritual state so well, he could affirm she was in a position to make it worthily. Her mother gave a willing consent, and she who had hoped against hope, learnt with grateful delight the surprising but not unexpected news, exclaiming repeatedly, 'I was quite sure, Lord, Thou wouldst grant my request, and that I was right to count on it.' When in after years she recalled this incident, it was always with indescribable sentiments of joy and happiness. She immediately began her preparation for that solemn and most important day by making a short retreat, in order to obtain the graces requisite for making her general confession. In this act the most considerable fault she could remember was her having made use of some unbecoming expressions, of which she did not at the time understand the true meaning. Though she felt considerable repugnance to repeating the actual words which she had used, she was determined to overcome her sense of shame. To her young imagination her contrition appeared insufficient if it were not accompanied with tears. She therefore spent two or three hours in trying to excite them, and was not satisfied till she had shed some. She afterwards took occasion from this little mistake to warn her religious against overstraining the sensitiveness of children.

When on a visit about this time to her grandmother, she heard some one say that the Franciscans gave themselves the discipline, whereupon she retired with one of her friends into another room to follow their example. They were, however, quite ignorant of the instrument used for the purpose, and proceeded to give the discipline to each other with the curtain ropes. Madame de Valori, growing uneasy at their prolonged absence, went in search of them, and was greatly surprised to find how they were occupied. On being questioned they naively answered, ‘That they were doing what the Franiscans did.’

Chapter II

Interior Trials and Physical sufferings. Henriette enters the Convent of the Sacred Heart. Her vow to Our Lady of La Delivrande.

Henriette's extreme delicacy of conscience and dread of offending God made her for a time over scrupulous, although her confessor observed and warned her against this danger. She no longer allowed herself the most ordinary relaxations of life, and was in the habit, when alone, of going up the stairs on her knees. Religious practices which had once seemed so delightful now gave her nothing but bitterness. Confession became a torment, owing to the aggravated importance which she gave to small faults. Unfortunately her confessor did not fully understand her mental state, and sharply reproved her for what he called 'resisting grace'. One day he went so far as to threaten that he would refuse her absolution if she continued as she was doing. This habitual strain of mind, which she supposed proper and necessary for her, caused her intense suffering, and injured her bodily health. More than this , her interior trials were sometimes so terrible that she was ready to give way to despair, and to abandon all further attempts. But she was supported in her weak moments, and fortified for the combat by that same God whose Spouse she was to become one day . This trial, however, lasted more than two years, and doubtless God permitted it in order that she, who was afterwards to guide so many souls along the spiritual path, might know by experience the different states through which it pleases Him to conduct those who devote themselves to His service, and might thus learn how to compassionate and assist them in their weakness.

The birth of her two brothers, by still straitening her father's income, rendered him doubly anxious about the future prospects of his family, and the restoration of the Bourbons having opened the way, he solicited employment, and was appointed to the lucrative post of Receiver General at Caen. Though he was obliged to borrow the 300,000 francs required as security, fortune smiled on him from that moment. Madame Dorcher, his aunt, one day asked him if he would accept her property on condition of paying her an annuity of 20,000 francs, as by this arrangement the family property might be kept entire. M. d'Osseville, after consulting with his immediate relatives, finally accepted her proposal, as being the only heir in a position to furnish the sum required. Madame Dorcher died two years later, and M. d'Osseville took possession of the fine property of Gavrus. This change of position was the means, under God, of restoring calm to Henriette's troubled soul. The priest to whom she applied on arriving at Caen quickly understood her spiritual state, and was able to restore her former confidence in God. The idea of entering the religious state was at this time frequently before her mind, but having a great dislike to it, she succeeded for a time in forcibly putting these thoughts aside.

As the position which Count d'Osseville now occupied obliged him to receive a good deal of company, Henriette had to appear more in society. In doing this, she found many fresh opportunities of practising mortification. Being the third daughter, she was sometimes a little passed over, more especially as her infirmity prevented her taking part in any active amusement. It also drew down little humiliations which were keenly felt by her, though she never allowed any sign of this to appear. In her later days, she confessed that she had never really been so indifferent to the remarks thus made as she professed to be at the time. In spite of her acute sufferings, her habitual amiability never deserted her, while the charm of her conversation never failed to attract many to her side. She especially sought the company of those who were left unnoticed by the rest, and her principle seems to have been to give much to others, and expect little for herself in return. Madame d'Osseville had herself superintended the education of her daughters at regular hours of the day, and as soon as she judged them capable of reflection, she had made it her study to develope their mental faculties. Her position gave her many opportunities of doing this, and after every entertainment given at home she examined them as to the effect produced on them by what they had seen, and heard in conversation, correcting any false impression they might have received, and thus guiding them to acquire just and sound views.

The habitual state of suffering in which Henriette passed her life, caused a depression of spirits which she tried to dissipate by reading works of fiction. Her delicate conscience was never fully at ease, notwithstanding the efforts made to reassure her, under the pretext that she stood in need of some relaxation of the kind. The promise she had made at her first Communion never to read novels, was always present to her mind. The books she was persuaded to read proved fatal to her piety by leading to many vain thoughts and the love of dress, and by giving her a distaste for religious exercises. Yet she never failed to frequent the sacraments. Sometimes at the moment of Holy Communion she experienced much interior trouble and a strong wish to draw back, until throwing herself at our Lord's feet, she protested that she would rather die than be guilty of sacrilege, and then her peace of mind generally returned. During three or four years of this kind of life, her health grew worse and worse, so that when she attained her eighteenth year, it was evident that the different plans which had been tried to remedy her deformity had only increased the evil. Her sufferings at this period were known only to God, but she confessed in later years that from childhood upwards she could not recall a single hour in which she had not had some bodily pain to offer to her Crucified

Lord. In addition to this she began to suffer from inflammation of the eyes, and was obliged to pass hours in a dark room. At length, in 1824, her doctor declared that from the advance which her complaint had made she could not possibly live six months longer. Her heart was forced out of its place towards the right side, and her left shoulder was drawn so far was to follow the orthopaedic treatment lately introduced into France. This proposal was a terrible blow for poor Henriette. While, on the one hand, she felt she had no right to refuse her consent to any plan suggested for prolonging her life, on the other she had a strong conscientious objection to enter any secular establishment not conducted on religious principles. On making known her feelings to Doctor Recamier, whom she had consulted, and knew to be a good Catholic, he reassured her most kindly, telling her that this particular treatment had been lately established at the Convent of the Sacré Coeur in the Rue de Varennes, Paris, and that the scapular which he has observed during his medical examination would ensure her an entrance there. After the removal of a slight difficulty, which arose from her being already twenty-one years of age, preparations were made for her leaving home. Many bitter tears were shed, both by her fond parents and by herself, for the separation was made doubly painful by the recent deaths of her two brothers and of her eldest sister, Cecilia, who at the early age of nineteen prayed that God would take her out of this world rather than that she should ever live to offend Him mortally. Her brother Edmund died while yet an infant, but Henry was old enough to be at the Jesuit College of St. Acheul, where the memory of his sanctity is preserved in the record of 'Edifying deaths', published by the Fathers. As Henriette's only remaining sister had been married to the Count de Jumilhac, her approaching departure would leave her parents quite alone.

Notwithstanding her generous acceptance of the sacrifice, Henriette, accustomed to all the charms of home life, and to the tender and assiduous care taken of her by her mother, had much to bear in her anticipation of the complete isolation, and the many privations she would have to undergo in her new position. Her parents intended, in the event of cure being wrought, to marry her to a cousin, who had been attached to her from youth, and who still pressed his suit, nowithstanding her deformity. But God had in His mercy far different designs regarding this soul which He destined for Himself. Mademoiselle d'Osseville entered the Convent of the Sacred Heart on August 17, 1824. The treatment under which she was now placed, and her distress of mind at being separated from her parents, greatly increased her physical sufferings, and to these God was pleased to add fresh interior trials. She underwent, we may truly say, a species of martyrdom, and it was from this period that she always dated her actual vocation to the religious state. The charity she met with from the whole community, and above all, from Madame de Marboeuf, widow of the famous general of that name, was a sign to her of the grace and peace which religion spreads as a balm over the sorrows of life. Her case being an exceptionally bad one, several new kinds of mechanism were tried, and her parents were put to very great expense, while she herself had to endure great agony. One day, when stretched on the bed mechanically contrived for her use she felt a cracking sensation pass through her frame, her body was at the same time drawn out, and her sides straightened, while her bodily and mental sufferings became so intense, that she fully believed herself on the point of death. In this extremity a sudden inspiration came over her to make a vow to Our Lady of La Delivrande, that she would go on pilgrimage to her shrine if she were graciously pleased to support her to the end of her course of treatment. She had hitherto only once visited the Sanctuary of La Delivrande,[1] and had hitherto directed all her petitions to Our Lady of Bon Secours, whose church is close to Rouen. But it was at La Delivrande that God had ordained His servant should found a community, though as yet she had no idea of such an undertaking. Her promise was accepted, and from that moment she felt strong and courageous, and in spite of the continuance of her pains, her general health was gradually restored by the successful application of the treatment.

The ladies following the same course of cure met only at meals, and showed little sympathy towards their new companion. Thus her first six weeks there were painful enough. But her gentle, amiable manners won their hearts, and disarmed the most prejudiced. At first her mother came daily, and spent some hours with her, but other duties soon required her to leave Paris. Madame de Marboeuf then came from time to time to pay her a short visit, and the rest of the day was passed by her in complete solitude. Stretched out by leather straps in an irksome position on her hard and curved bed, she offered up to God the wearisome sameness of her attitude and the monotony of her existence. And He more than made up to her the loss of human consolation by holding communion with her heart, and to draw her more effectually to Himself, enabled her to join in a retreat given in December of the same year. During this retreat she deeply lamented her past faults, and renewed the promises made at her first Communion.

The anxiety of mind from which she still continued to suffer is attributable to the imprudence of her confessor, who seeing how capable she was of attaining to high perfection, hindered the work by trying to push her on too rapidly. She was advised to consult Father Druilhet, a Jesuit, and finding her peace of mind quite restored after a general confession made to him, and observing that God had given him a special light to understand her state, she placed herself entirely under his direction. He completed what the retreat had so well begun, and fixed her purpose steadfastly to renounce for ever all that savoured of the world, and to give herself wholly up to the service of God. It was in the Convent of the Sacred Heart that Henriette's devotion to her Angel

1 An account of this sanctuary will be found in a note at the end of this chapter.

Guardian became especially marked. She delighted in relating instances of his special protection: how when longing for Madame de Marboeuf's company, she begged her good angel to go and bring her, or when anything fell which her constrained position would not admit of her picking up, she asked her Angel Guardian to send Mademoiselle d'Hendecourt to her, and on every occasion the favour was granted. After the lapse of fifteen months Henriette's father resolved on bringing her home, and continuing there the system of cure so happily commenced in the convent. On her return to Gavrus, her friends found her as totally changed in disposition as she was in external appearance. The love of piety and serious occupation now reigned supreme in her, and God alone could satisfy her heart. So much had her character been confirmed in grace, that Madame de Grammont remarked she would venture to place her at the head of one of her largest houses.

Henriette began to busy herself in every good work which her position allowed her to undertake, and she sought out in the bosom of her own family a real friend, to whom she might confide her thoughts. Such a one she found in her aunt, Madame de Valori, who afterwards became her spiritual daughter, under the name of Mother St. Anne of the Passion. These two future religious worked in concert to extend through the diocese of Bayeux, the lately instituted association for the Propagation of the Faith, and God so blessed their endeavours that within eighteen months they raised the subscriptions from only three or four hundred francs to the large sum of eight thousand. On Sunday she was fond of assembling the young girls of the village, and teaching them how to occupy their time piously and pleasantly, and they, on their part regarded her as a saint, wondering that her sufferings never impaired the cheerful gaiety which endeared her so much to them. A few months only passed before she began to form more definite desires of entering into religion, and the miraculous cure of her sister, Madame de Jumilhac, which happened at this time, filled her parents with such profound gratitude to the Blessed Virgin, that they were ready to make any sacrifice in her honour.

NOTE

LA DELIVRANDE, with which place the foundation by Mother St. Mary of the religious Congregation of the 'Faithful Virgin' is so intimately connected, is a large village, or rather a small town, of some twelve hundred inhabitants, containing a very ancient and famous shrine of Our Lady, close to the sea-coast, and is situated about seven miles to the north-west of Caen, in Normandy. The very situation of this old-fashioned 'bourg' within a district of France so much associated with the early history of England, adds much to the interest which we feel in the introduction into this country of an institution so thoroughly of Norman growth, and the neighbourhood of La Delivrande abounds with curious memorials of the possession of the country by the English, not only in the famous Church of St. Pierre at Caen, but in the parishes of Bernières, Langrunes, St.Aubin, and others, each of which possesses a beautiful old church with a magnificent spire, the design of English architects and the work of English hands, and originally intended to mark out the boundaries of a city which was never built. It has been observed, also, that the Norman patois, especially about Caen, contains many English words.

There seems abundance of authority for tracing back the history of the shrine and pilgrimage of La Delivrande to St. Regnobert, Bishop of Bayeux, who lived in the seventh century, and died about the year 666. The town itself has sprung up from the fame of the statue and chapel of our Lady, although its name is scarcely to be taken as etymologically the expression of confidence in Mary's protection, but as a modern form of *Dell' Yorande* (Livandria), or of a name compounded of the English word *dell* (existing in Normandy) and *Yorande*, the latter opinion being probably suggested by the modern prefix of *la* the full name *La Delivrande*. Besides its Norman origin, we trace a fresh interest and significance in the fact that along this northern coast of Gaul, ravaged successively by the Saxons, the Angles and Jutes, St. Regnobert may be considered as the Apostle of the Saxons in his diocese. He erected several churches amongst them, which were doubtless the scenes, not only of many conversations, but of many miracles granted to dispel heathen darkness and idolatry. To such graces as these are to be attributed the birth of a devotion and pilgrimage to our Lady at La Delivrande which was destined to go on, ever reviving from its temporary extinction, and ever increasing in popularity, and to be the cradle of a congregation of religious who would cross over into England, to help to save Catholic orphans from the evils of English Protestant workhouses. According to Robert Cénalis, Bishop of Avranches in 1552, St. Regnobert was a Count of Dessin, in the same part of the country, and devoted all his temporal goods to the enriching of his cathedral, and of La Delivrande, together with his other foundations.

In the course of time the Normans ravaged the district and burnt down the chapel of La Delivrande, as well as other churches, and since in the ninth century they made their work complete by destroying all the records they could find, the history of this shrine remains a blank from the seventh to the close of the eleventh century. In the year 1050 the ruined chapel was restored by a certain Beaudoin, whom earlier chronicles make to have been a nobleman of the country, and Baron of Douvres, but whom a modern authority claims as Beaudouin, Lord of Reviers, the owner of large possessions in England. With this restoration a very interesting pious legend is connected.

A shepherd of the land of Reviers remarked that a particular sheep in his flock frequently turned aside from the rest to visit a spot close to their pasture ground, and that it tried to dig up the ground with its foot and with its horn, lying down in the same place when too tired to continue its laborious work. As he further observed that though this sheep ate nothing it retained all the appearance of being as well fed as the others, he told the Count of so wonderful a phenomenon. The soil thus partially dug up was immediately removed, and the long-buried statue of the Blessed Virgin was brought to light, in the presence of the lord of the manor, and of all the gentlemen and people from the country round. The Count, recognizing this indication of the Divine will, rebuilt and founded a chapel on the spot, placed the statue in a decorated niche, and consigned its charge to the cathedral chapter of Bayeux. The statue itself is only about three feet in height, and the head of our Lady was at one time encircled by diadem of carved stone work, which had been mutilated either by the Normans, or by the Protestants in 1562; the whole figure indicates a debased style of sculpture, and therefore belongs to the period of the middle ages. The chapel has been much altered and patched up at different times, but evidently dates from the eleventh or twelfth century. However incongruous and bad in taste these supposed improvements were, they showed the care and interest taken in the shrine.

Ever since the beginning of the thirteenth century La Delivrande has been the centre of devotion to constant succession of pilgrims, nor did the Bishops of Bayeux take possession of their Episcopal see before they had made a pilgrimage to La Delivrande. The greater number of parishes throughout the diocese made their annual processions to our Lady's Chapel as a regular custom, and it gradually became filled to overflowing with ex votos in acknowledgment of favours granted; many a legacy too was left and donation made to it. Our Lady's shrine has also been visited by royal pilgrims, for on the 14th of August, 1473, Louis the Eleventh of France arrived there in great state, and assisted at the High Mass on the feast of the Assumption. He made an offering, and added a new altar to the chapel, and departed again on the 19th. Louis the Thirteenth afterwards followed his example. Towards the beginning of the sixteenth century, priests crowded hither to say Mass before the shrine, and the pilgrims became to so numerous that it was found necessary to draw up a list of regulations, for the purpose of maintaining order amongst them. Indeed, the gifts presented multiplied so rapidly that the visitors were forbidden to put them up themselves, without having first obtained leave to do so. Masses were said in succession at five different altars and thirteen silver lamps burnt constantly before the shrine. It could not be expected that so rich and celebrated a centre of devotion should escape the sacrilegious hatred and rapacity of the Revolutionists of 1793. In that year the statue was carried off to Caen, and remained there till 1802. Meanwhile the emptied chapel was left closed without any further dishonour being done to it; and it was amidst transports of joy from all the surrounding neighbourhood that the statue, itself also intact, was borne in triumph to its former resting-place. Soon the chapel of our Lady was readorned, and refilled with crowds of worshippers to the number of from one hundred thousand to one hundred and fifty thousand pilgrims every year. In 1834, Mgr.de Quélen, Archbishop of Paris, came in pilgrimage to the plain and old-fashioned little chapel, an act which he often repeated; and in 1838 he brought a new statue, which, in return for a great favour granted, he had vowed to our Lady as 'The faithful Virgin.' Having blessed it, he had it transferred to its final site in the convent and orphanage of La Charité. Since this event a beautiful little Gothic chapel has been built for our Lady of La Delivrande, and the old statue has been solemnly crowned.

Chapter III

Henriette at Langrunes. Mission at Gavrus. She chooses Father Saulet as her director.

Shortly after the events which we have just mentioned Count d`Osseville, having heard of the difficulties experienced by the Reverend Fathers of the mission in completing the buildings at La Delivrande for want of funds, gladly came forward and provided the necessary amount. He little foresaw the consequences of a step, which introduced Henriette to the acquaintance of that spiritual guide who was afterwards to cooperate with her in the foundation of the community of La Delivrande. In the month of February, 1827, Father Saulet, Superior of the mission, passed through Caen, and feeling desirous to thank M. d`Osseville personally for his generous aid, he willingly accepted the offer made to him to sleep at Gavrus. Notwithstanding his grave, imposing appearance, Henriette felt drawn towards him as she had been to no other except Father Druilhet. An opportunity presenting itself of speaking alone with him, as they stood in the embrasure of a window, she opened her heart to him on the subject of her vocation, and the wish which she then had to enter the Convent of the Sacred Heart. As if under a sudden inspiration, he answered her quickly: 'Why should you leave your own diocese? Is there not La Delivrande and the Blessed Virgin?' 'But what can I do at La Delivrande, where there is no religious house?' she replied in surprise. 'Speak however of it to our Blessed Mother, and if she wants me, come for me'. For the next eighteen months the words which she had uttered, almost passed from her recollection; yet not entirely, for when she made any steps towards entering the Sacred Heart Convent, they vaguely recurred to her mind.

Interior struggles and uncertainty as to her vocation began to attack her again, and as her parents intended passing some time with her at Langrunes for sea-bathing, she thought this a good opportunity for asking leave to make a second retreat. They looked upon it as a novelty , and dissuaded her from it. She passed the six weeks at Langrunes quietly with her aunt, the Countess de Valori, who herself requested Father Saulet to preach them a short retreat of three days.

In a previous visit Henriette had consulted him upon the point of conquering her pride, and though he scarcely knew her, yet understanding at once the work which God had begun in her generous soul, he exclaimed: 'Pride! You Proud! Tell me, I beg of you, what you can have to be proud of?' These words he uttered in a tone of such surprise and conviction of their truth, that the poor girl was struck dumb, and for a long while felt quite cured of her self-love. At the same time this frank simplicity only added to the confidence with which he had inspired her. During the short retreat under him she entered fully into the details of her past life and present dispositions, and in hearing these he positively assured her that she was called to the religious state, but that, as he did not consider the time for this step had yet come, she was to decline to follow the advice of her ordinary confessor, who wished her to enter the Novitiate of the Sacred Heart Convent, after leaving Langrunes. His decision threw her into great embarrassment; but God, seeing her sincere desire simply to do His holy will, provided help for her in Father Drouilhet who, when accompanying his Provincial into Brittany, happened to pass through Caen. Though he had only a few hours at his disposal, he consented to go as far as Langrunes to see her. After he had heard the recital of all that was passing in her soul, he too was of opinion that she should not enter religion immediately, but await the course of God's providence.

Whilst still at the sea-side Father Saulet often visited her, and about the same time a little incident occurred which caused her much humiliation. Her parents had presented a bell to La Delivrande, and the ceremony of baptizing it was to take place in the Church. Henriette greatly disliked appearing with crutches in public, so after praying a long time before the Blessed Virgin's statue, she quietly withdrew from the Church, just as the crowd came in. But when she heard afterwards what Father Saulet had preached, she bitterly reproached herself, as she had not heard a sermon since she was at the Convent of the Sacred Heart. On her expressing her disappointment, the Father did not allow so good an opportunity of mortifying her pride to escape. 'How?' he exclaimed before all the company present; 'was it on account of your infirmity that you went out? I thought you were above such littleness. I hope God will always punish you in this manner for the like faults.'

He promised before leaving Langrunes to hear her confession at her uncle's house, some miles from La Deliverande, and finding her crushed beneath the sorrows and crosses with which God was then trying her sincerity, he showed her a picture of our Lord in the Garden of Olives and said : 'He drank the bitterest contents of the chalice. Some drops remain. He offers them to you. Will you reject them?' This appealed to her faith, restored her drooping courage, but the interior struggle had been so violent that her health was seriously affected. Her father on coming to see her soon after was so struck with the change in her appearance that he at once took her back to Gavrus, and she had scarcely arrived when a fresh severe illness reduced her to the brink of the grave, and though the danger was averted, she passed the next year in a very weak state. A fortnight after her attack, Father Saulet and several other priests gave a mission at Gavrus, which was attended with great success. The Fathers lived at the château, and the Superior, in order to prevent overtaxing their strength, placed them under obedience to the Count, being unable himself to remain. The virtues which they practised, and their childlike submission to their temporary Superior, made a deep impression on all the family.

In spite of her sufferings Mademoiselle d`Osseville attended the exercises of the mission, and even instructed some old women whose ignorance prevented their admission to the sacraments. One of them had never heard the mysteries of the Incarnation and Redemption related in detail, a mark of the state of things shortly after the Revolution. When her pious teacher told her of the prodigies of Divine love, the poor woman flung herself on her neck exclaiming: 'Ah! Mademoiselle, why, if everyone only knew this, there would be no living person in the world, people would be crying all day long.' Uncouthness of manner never repulsed Henriette, whose zeal and kindness in imparting instruction often drew from her pupils, on leaving her, warm expressions of admiration. This apostolate, however consoling to her faith, was not without great trials to her patience from the difficulty of making her aged hearers understand the truths of religion. On one Good Friday her description of the events of our Lord's Passion moved an old lady to tears of ready sympathy. But the following year came a change. When she spoke to the same old woman she was listened to with marked indifference, and on inquiring the reason, only got for answer: 'La! Mademoiselle, why do you keep going over the same story again? I cried over it last year, but why did He let Himself be caught again?.'

At the conclusion of a retreat given shortly after the mission of Gavrus, one of the missioners, M. le Herpeur (afterwards Bishop of Martinique), confided five young girls to her care, begging her to train them in the spiritual life; of these two afterwards became religious at La Delivrande. When she expressed a doubt of having capacity for the work, he replied in an almost prophetic tone: 'God by giving you the charge of this little community is preparing you for what He intends later on'. She assembled her young ones the very next day, and was so much delighted with their simplicity, that wishing to give M. le Herpeur the pleasure of sharing her first success, she invited him after a few days to come and hear them make their meditation aloud. When they had concluded, he insisted on her doing the same herself, and this, she afterwards confessed, was far harder for her to do in obedience to him, than it had been for her pious scholars. She placed her little flock under the protection of Mary Immaculate, for whom she taught them to cherish a tender devotion. Seeing the condition of the altar of our Lady in the church at Gavrus, she longed to undertake its complete restoration, but her purse had been emptied for the poor and the Propagation of the Faith, and she did not like to apply again so soon to her father. What could she do? An expedient suggested itself, and her generous heart quickly adopted it. She took a collection of foreign coins of considerable value, a gift which she prized, and hurrying with it to the church laid it on the altar of Mary, saying: `There, dear Mother, I have nothing else, but at least this is for you'. As she returned joyfully home, she met her father, who, wishing to make her a present similar to that which he had just given her sister, placed 1200 francs in her hand to use it as she pleased. This unexpected gift seemed to her faithful servant to come direct from the hands of Mary, and in her joy and gratitude towards her Mother in Heaven she almost forgot to thank her kind father. Three hundred francs afterwards added to the sum, gave her more than enough to put the little chapel in order, and she gave the care of it to her small community, now increased by the admission of seven new members.

During the retreat above alluded to, Father Saulet showed Henriette a letter from a rich lady, in which she expressed her desire of retiring to La Delivrande and founding a work of charity there. This person had already spoken to the Countess de Valori, who wished much to procure a Christian education for the children of the village, but was far from imagining at the time that she was herself destined to be one of the foundation stones of the establishment.

Henriette felt her soul stirred within her as she returned the letter, and calling to mind her first interview with the Father Superior, she could not help exclaiming: 'This is my work, Father; it is mine.' The Superior wishing further to try her, coldly replied: 'What have you to do with a work that does not exist? I forbid you to think of it. I only permit you to pray for it'. Obedient and docile as usual that gentle soul submitted; but thenceforth all other thought but that of a community at La Delivrande threw her soul into a state of trouble and perplexity. At a later period she declared to her daughters that the idea of founding an orphanage near Mary's chosen sanctuary had often presented itself to her, though only to be dismissed as a foolish fancy.

From the moment that a foundress thus offered herself, the thought of becoming a religious grew stronger, and the longer she prayed the more did that confidence increase which was to support her through all the trials and opposition she afterwards encountered in the fulfilment of God's will. Waiting patiently for the time marked out by His providence, she continued to be the Mother of the poor at Gavrus, especially for little children, for whom she had always a kind word or a caress. Thus her life passed on, sanctified by charity and suffering.

Chapter IV

Henriette at Langrunes and at Paris. She retires to the convent of the Sacred Heart, and seeks a suitable house for her Foundation.

Towards the middle of the summer of 1828 Mademoiselle d`Osseville went again to Langrunes with her aunt and the Countess of Valori. She had just left her ordinary confessor, to follow exclusively the guidance of Father Saulet, when the latter was seized with brain fever which within two days threatened his life. His illness caused general dismay throughout the neighbourhood; prayers and novenas were made in all directions, yet the danger became only more imminent. The Countess de Valori and her niece were not among the least fervent suppliants for his recovery. On the 8th of July, when all hope seemed lost, the thought of an orphanage at La Delivrande struck each separately, and without communicating their impression to each other, they simultaneously knelt down and made a vow to offer up their hearts as a perpetual oblation of love and gratitude to their Holy Mother. They both rose with the inward assurance that their prayer had been heard, and that the Blessed Virgin would obtain the cure of the venerated Father, who for more than twenty years was to be their guide and stay. Nor were their hopes deceived. Father Saulet recovered in a few days, but several years passed before he knew of the offering that had been made.

Some time after his recovery the Father went to pay them a visit, and the projected work was spoken of. It seemed then almost hopeless, for the lady who had first proposed the idea had since abandoned it, and taken a decided step in another direction. 'What are we to do?' said Father Saulet to the Countess de Valori; 'there is no one left but Mademoiselle d`Osseville, and though she is always tormenting me on the subject, she is too young'. Henriette listened in silence for her aunt's reply, divided between the fear of undertaking such a responsibility and the struggling consciousness of a vocation. After brief reflection, as in the presence of God, the Countess replied that she felt sure Henriette would prove quite capable of directing the proposed foundation. Father Saulet then decided that the month which was to elapse before the departure of the family for Paris, should be spent in prayer, after which the whole matter was to be laid before Father Druilhet, and his decision accepted as final. Meantime no mention should be made of it, even to the other members of the family.

In the month of September, 1828, Mademoiselle d`Osseville repaired to Paris, where the Countess de Valori shortly after, unexpectedly joined her, to be a comfort and support amidst new difficulties. Henriette hastened to consult

Father Druilhet, laying before him all that had passed since their former interview. At first he heard what she had to say with marked reserve, but after several interviews he advised her to attend a spiritual retreat, given at the Convent of the Sacred Heart by the celebrated Father M'Carthy. His object evidently was to re-awaken her old attraction towards that order, the retreat being devoted to an explanation of the spirit of its Institute. But God ordained that a totally contrary effect should be produced by her retreat, so that with all her veneration and esteem for the Institute of the Sacred Heart, Mademoiselle d`Osseville entirely abandoned the idea of herself belonging to it. Seeing this, Father Druilhet questioned his penitent still more closely as to the details of the proposed undertaking at La Delivrande. This course greatly distressed Henriette, as she had been strictly forbidden by Father Saulet to let her mind dwell on plans for the future, and she had faithfully obeyed him. The Countess de Valori advised her to beg Father Saulet to come to Paris, and himself talk over the matter with Father Druilhet. And although Father Saulet came, and had several interviews with Father Druilhet, who learnt to esteem him as a saint, their conversations produced no result, and the Father Superior returned to Normandy, leaving the decision in Father Druilhet's hands. The latter, wishing much that his spiritual daughter should enter the Sacred Heart Convent, yet afraid of opposing God's will, which seemed to call her elsewhere, directed her to begin a novena for the more perfect recovery of her health, and to say to God with all simplicity: 'In the name of the obedience, I owe Father Druilhet, I beg You to restore to me my health.' His intention was, as he afterwards acknowledged, that had this prayer been granted, he would have persuaded her immediately to enter the Sacred Heart Convent.

The night before the novena was to begin; Henriette woke up at mid-night with a burning fever and a sudden attack of violent inflammation. Other severe symptoms appeared during the novena, and she was at the close worse than she had been before; indeed, it was observed that the direction of her mind to the thought of entering the Institute of the Sacred Heart increased her illness, whereas the thought of commencing the work at La Delivrande invariably made her better. The perplexity of Father Druilhet was great, and he remarked, 'I see in you two different vocations, for I have long believed you were decidedly called to the Congregation of the Sacred Heart, and now you are drawn strongly to La Delivrande. Permit me to consult the Superioress General of the nuns of the Sacred Heart.' Leave being granted, a day was fixed for receiving her answer, but when the anxious moment came, Henriette found only a letter left by Father Druilhet to say that he had been suddenly called away to preach a retreat in a distant town; he, however, bade her to go to the Mother Supcrioress, who would tell her what had been decided on. Henriette therefore repaired to the Sacred Heart Convent, when, after waiting several hours, she was told that the Reverend Mother was too busy to see her that day.

For several successive days she repeated her call, but to no purpose; God permitting these delays in order to increase her virtue and merit. When at last the long wished for interview was granted, it only added to her perplexity; for the Reverend Mother, after questioning her, gave her to understand that she feared she was resisting grace in not entering the Order of the Sacred Heart, and was prompted only by her self-will and private tastes in wishing to found a house at La Delivrande. Henriette withdrew with a heart full of anguish, and for a whole week she found her only comfort at the feet of her Holy Mother, assuring her that she sought but to do the will of her Divine Son. To complete her embarrassment, the physicians declared that it was unnecessary for her to remain longer in Paris, and Count d´Osseville resolved to return at once into Normandy. All now appeared lost; but God, Who never forsakes those who abandon all to Him, permitted that Father Druilhet should return to Paris just as Henriette´s anxiety reached its height. He was surprised at the result of the interview, for he had agreed with the Superioress that as Mademoiselle d´Osseville´s vocation for La Delivrande was so strong, she should be allowed to try it, and only if it failed should she be asked to join the Order of the Sacred Heart. He saw, however, in all that had passed the special action of Providence and a presage of the future work which God designed to effect through one whom He permitted to be thus tried. He put a speedy end to her uncertainty by the words, 'Go, my daughter, where God leads you. All I ask is, that though you direct your mind towards that end, you should take no definite step for one year'.

Father Saulet now judged that the time had come for making known to her parents their daughter´s vocation to establish a house at La Delivrande. He found them full of that lively faith and generous self-sacrifice which they continued throughout to display, but yet somewhat alarmed at the greatness of the undertaking and at the many obstacles to be overcome before its happy accomplishment. It was decided that the Bishop should be consulted, and that search should be made for a suitable house, while in the meantime Mademoiselle d´Osseville was to pass a few weeks in the Convent of La Charité at Bayeux to study the practice of the religious life. At first all seemed to favour the designs of the young foundress. The proposal to begin a convent near the venerated sanctuary of our Blessed Lady was received with great favour by the Bishop, though at the same time the special interest he took in the Community of Bayeux made him prefer that Henriette should become a religious of their house rather than undertake a new foundation. This proposal she respectfully but firmly declined. His Lordship would not give up his idea, and hence the many crosses which through long years oppressed the Institute. At the same time Monseigneur Dancel readily consented that Mademoiselle d´Osseville should be admitted to the novitiate in the convent of his episcopal town, and told the Superior that he wished Henriette, though still a secular, to be initiated into the most intimate details of the religious life, and even to be present at the meetings of the Council and the Chapter.

Accompanied by a young friend, also destined for the work before her, she arrived at Bayeux on the 3rd of February, 1829. The six weeks she passed at that time in the convent were marked by the most abundant heavenly consolations, granted by her Heavenly Father to strengthen her for the coming storm. She admired the virtue of the Superioress, and spared nothing to fit herself for the duties of the life she was about to embrace. The Bishop treated her with uniform kindness during her stay at the convent, and, finding her determined, sent her at her departure an autograph authorization to found at La Delivrande an institution under the title of the 'Poor Orphans of Mary'. Every one seemed disposed to cooperate in the execution of a design which was to contribute so much to the glory of God. Henriette's heart was full of joy: she seemed already to have reached the long wished for goal, when the devil, ever jealous of good, tried by fresh artifices to ruin her enterprise. The Mother Superioress and the confessor of the convent at Bayeux, suggested to Mademoiselle d'Osseville, as a means of facilitating her enterprise, that she should present to the Government the statutes of their own order as those of her foundation. This proposal Henriette accepted, reserving to herself, as she was advised to do, the right of changing, in concert with Father Saulet, any point she thought advisable in the rules and constitutions. In accepting this offer she little anticipated how much sorrow and contradiction would arise from it. She saw in the step only an act of generous and disinterested kindness which touched her own noble heart.

The first object Mademoiselle d'Osseville had in view, on returning to her family, was to find a spot near La Delivrande fitted for a community. But now all those on whose aid she had trusted, thwarted her designs. Some recommended her to buy an old Ursuline convent at Caen; others suggested that she should restore the fine old Abbey of Ardennes, half a league from the town; while Count d'Osseville, who was ready enough to make the sacrifice demanded of his fortune, blinded by his love for his daughter, begged her to establish herself in a walled enclosure in his own park, where he promised to build whatever she wished. But God had made known His will, and she would listen to none of these suggestions, making only fresh efforts to find a house near La Delivrande , to which place she came with the other members of her family, at the end of Lent, 1829, to attend a retreat of eight days.

Father Saulet now began to make her taste humiliation, in order to acquire the virtue of humility, on which he wished specially to found the new convent at La Delivrande; at the same time he introduced to her several young persons desirous of joining her in her new foundation, and of confiding their souls to her care. After some stay in her family, Henriette came to Langrunes for sea-bathing , which her health still rendered necessary, and, while there, devoted herself to good works in visiting the sick and poor.

About this time an incident occurred which shows the manner in which the Father Superior formed her to obedience. Mademoiselle d´Osseville mentioned to him one morning that she and her aunt were going on the following day to La Delivrande , and would pay a visit to the young women's workroom. 'People don't go there for nothing,' rejoined the Father, 'so you will speak to them of God, and each give them a little exhortation.' The Countess ventured to expostulate, but Henriette simply asked if he was serious in what he said. 'Yes, quite serious', he replied, 'it is my decided wish.' They prepared to obey, and began to look out for a subject, Henriette making her aunt promise to speak first, while they agreed to divide the subject between them, the aunt taking the first part and her niece the second. The next day they came to La Delivrande, more dead than alive, and, after earnestly imploring the help of Mary, proceeded to the workroom. Their surprise was great on seeing the curé of a neighbouring parish, who had also come to visit the lace -makers. 'Ah', thought Henriette, with a sigh of relief, 'I am rid of my sermon for today, at any rate;' but to her great disappointment the young people told her that Father Superior had promised them an address, and this the priest who was present insisted upon their giving. Henriette expected her aunt to begin, but she pleaded illness, and laid the whole burden on her niece, who, as all knelt down, with beating heart and burning cheeks recited the *Veni Sancte Spiritus*, and then began her exhortation. In this she experienced the strength which obedience gives, for, as she afterwards said, she never spoke with greater ease or freedom.

In the meantime the Count hoped he had at last succeeded in finding a suitable house, when, on the day fixed for signing the contract, the proprietor drew back, and the affair was broken off. That at least her time might not be lost, Henriette determined after the bathing season to return to the convent of La Charité at Bayeux, and wait the hour fixed by Providence. Father Saulet wrote to the Bishop and Mother Superior on the subject, and both joyfully consented to the proposal. Just then Mademoiselle d´Hendecourt, who was about to enter the Congregation of the Sacred Heart, came to bid her old friend farewell, and at the same time Madame de Valori received a letter from her niece, Mademoiselle de l´Espinasse, announcing her speedy arrival for the bathing season. Though this visit seemed ill-timed, as the family had but a few days to spend together, they could not help feeling that the circumstances might be providential, and so in fact they were. A day or two after their arrival, Father Saulet consented to preach them a little retreat, on condition that Henriette should supply his place when he was otherwise occupied. A blessing attended her words which frequently drew tears from her hearers, and they determined to follow the guidance of God. Being strongly drawn towards the work at La Delivrande, Mademoiselle d´Hendecourt gave up all intention of entering as a nun of the Sacred Heart, and, along with some other young ladies, placed herself under the care of Mademoiselle d´Osseville to be formed for the religious life.

Henriette and her aunt examined several religious rules with a view to prepare the constitutions she wished to give to her new Institute, and the Father Superior promised to revise her work from time to time. Though this was partly done, it was not till the year 1848 that Mother St. Mary could complete the work of which she had conceived the plan nineteen years before. Another consolation was granted her at this period. As her friend Mademoiselle de l´Espinasse had heard nothing of Henriette´s projects, Father Saulet thought it right she should be made acquainted with them; and she was at once so delighted with an idea entirely corresponding to the wish of her own heart, that she exclaimed: 'Until now I have said nothing of my intention of being a religious, and I was uncertain which house to choose; but now I am decided, and I beg of you to consider me among your daughters.' Thenceforth Mademoiselle de l´Espinasse gave Mademoiselle d´Osseville the title of 'Mother'.

Chapter V

Henriette returns to Bayeux. Her sufferings during her novitiate. Her illness. Her clothing.

On the feast of the Assumption the whole family of Mademoiselle d′Osseville went in pilgrimage to Our Lady of La Delivrande, and it was then that the Blessed Virgin bestowed on her daughter one of the most precious favours she had yet received. Prostrate at the feet of the miraculous image, Henriette found herself unable to follow the Vespers which were being chanted. Her mind, filled with thoughts of her future community, felt crushed beneath the difficulties and delays that seemed to multiply around her, and ill and tired as she was, she knew not what subject to take for her meditation. When in all simplicity she asked our Lady to suggest one to her, she suddenly heard within her heart the words *Virgo Fidelis*, and saw interiorly depicted in her mind with great vividness the fidelity of the Blessed and Immaculate Virgin towards all who trust in her. The work she was to accomplish was represented to her, together with all the obstacles that now or later on were to impede it, yet at the same time no doubt was left as to its ultimate success through the aid of Mary, who would ever prove to this Institute the Faithful Virgin. Her Superiors, struck by the favours afterwards obtained through the invocation of our Lady under the title of "Faithful Virgin," decided that the Reverend Mother should not allow her daughters to remain in ignorance of the promise made to her in behalf of them, and they have since been witnesses of its exact accomplishment on many occasions.

Before leaving La Delivrande to return to the Convent of La Charité at Bayeux, Henriette and her future nuns wished to place at the feet of our Lady some testimony of their love and confidence. As it was settled that the community which they wished to found should specially devote itself to the education of poor orphans, they chose the picture of a little shivering child, which had been given to Henriette by a girl of ten years of age, who said she wanted to present her with her first orphan. Father Saulet entered into the idea, and the little picture was framed and laid on the altar while he offered the Holy Sacrifice of the Mass to consecrate his spiritual daughters to God through Mary. After Mass he hung it up close to the statue of the Blessed Virgin, that she might, as he said, continually hear the voice of the little orphan pleading for the work. Within a day or two Henriette bade her home and family a last farewell. Her parents, though resigned, felt the departure of their beloved daughter severely. Henriette assembled the servants and begged them to pardon the bad example and trouble she had given them—being much attached to her they only answered by their tears and sobs. The Father Superior celebrated Mass on the morning of her departure, September 3, 1829, and all the family received Holy Communion, seeking strength and consolation for the sacrifice that was now at hand. After the first moments given to mutual sorrow, following upon the trying scenes which they had passed through, Father Saulet gradually led back the thoughts of Henriette and Mademoiselle d'Hendecourt and a young friend who accompanied her, to the oblation which they made of themselves to God, and after reciting some devotions together, they began to discuss with cheerfulness their future projects.

On their arrival at Bayeux, the Mother Superior placed on the very threshold the postulant's veil over Mademoiselle d'Osseville's head, as the Bishop had decided that the six weeks passed there in February should count as part of her noviceship. Her arrival was a source of rejoicing for the whole house. The boarders who had been the objects of her solicitude on her previous visit rushed to embrace her, and the religious expressed their great satisfaction. In the evening she had a long interview with Father Saulet, who again consoled her on the late separation, gave her careful directions how to become a really holy religious, and told her that the Mother Superior wished she should, during the first six months, dismiss the thought of La Delivrande from her mind, in order to turn her whole attention to the practice of the religious life, adding, 'I myself see nothing but advantage in such an act of self -denial, and forbid you to think of future plans except when the interests of the work require your entering upon the subject with your family.' With this prohibition Henriette at once complied. A short time afterwards, the young person from La Delivrande who was to attend on Henriette as long as she continued the orthopaedic treatment, yielding to a sudden temptation, left the convent, and Mademoiselle d'Hendecourt, having finished her retreat, was obliged to return home. She had not yet obtained her father's consent to become a religious, but in her earnest desire to join her friend, and render her the little services necessary for her, she made another effort, strengthened by a vow to the Blessed Virgin at La Delivrande, and against all human probability her father's consent was at last given, and she entered the novitiate on September 14, 1829.

Father Saulet required at Henriette's admission, first that her letters to him should be sent without being read, and to this the Bishop consented; secondly, that she should be allowed to see and communicate freely with any one who came to offer herself for the future work at La Delivrande. The convent of La Charité at Bayeux had been destroyed during the Revolution, and was only just rising from its ruins. The poverty of the religious being extreme, they had not sufficient covering to protect them from the cold winter nights, and were obliged to use their choir cloaks. They could only get a few bits of green wood with which to light their fire, while at the same time the house was in a ruinous and dilapidated state. Several of the nuns wore cotton habits, not having the means of procuring serge. These details reveal to us how much the young postulant, accustomed to the comforts of affluence, had to undergo; but her fidelity and self-denial were unfailing, and it was perhaps her ready acceptance of outward privation that won for her so much consolation and so strong a love of poverty. One Sunday at Vespers she was so fatigued that she asked to be dispensed from singing, and to be allowed to read instead. Permission was refused, and she was told that if she could not chant, she at least could meditate. Being incapable of an hour's mental application, she meekly turned to our Lord and said in the deep filial confidence of her heart: 'I come to rest my head on Your knees, since I am too ill to meditate.' Scarcely had she thus spoken when her good Lord appeared to her and granted her this favour, while He filled her soul with His sweetest consolations. Fearing this might have been an illusion of the devil, she gave an account of it to her Superiors, who reassured her, saying that it came from God alone, and was the presage of crosses in the future. She made herself very useful in the community, the Superiors of which were most anxious to retain her. To the externs and boarders she gave instruction, seated in her mechanical chair, and made herself so beloved that several families withdrew their children from other houses to confide them to her care. Towards the month of October her health again declined, and her life was even despaired of, but on receiving Holy Communion she was pronounced out of danger. Her illness lasted three weeks, but the arrival of Father Saulet and the joy of receiving the religious habit on November 27, 1829, contributed much to her recovery. She chose St. Mary for her name in religion, and Father Saulet preached very appropriately from the text, 'Mary hath chosen the better part, which shall not be taken from her.'

CHAPTER VI

Purchase of a House at La Delivrande. Henriette receives her first orphan. Delay in leaving Bayeux. Her profession.

Shortly after the ceremony of clothing, Count d'Osseville had an interview with the King, Charles X, and spoke to him of his daughter's wish to found a community at La Delivrande. The King strongly approved of the project, and promised to recognize it as soon as established. On hearing this good news from her father, Henriette hastened to communicate it to the Superior, not doubting but that she would congratulate her on it. Her surprise and perplexity were excessive when she heard only bitter complaints and reproaches for still harbouring thoughts about La Delivrande, and for having made a secret of them during so many months. She replied with all humility that, while her intentions were unchanged, silence had been expressly enjoined on her by the Superior herself. But we cannot enter into the details of all she had to undergo during the months which followed, though many of them are preserved in the annals of the house. At first Father Saulet visited her frequently, to support her in the painful conflict with those who sought to detain her; but he soon plainly saw that her painful position could be terminated only by the immediate foundation of La Delivrande, and he advised Henriette to press this point upon her parents. The Count happening to come to see his daughter remarked her sadness, and inquired if she was contented with her new life. His question led to a partial explanation, and the moment she confessed that all unhappiness would be at an end if she were in La Delivrande, Count d'Osseville promised to find a house for her there, and to make the necessary arrangements at all costs. Father Saulet then caused several novenas to be offered up for the success of the undertaking, and Henriette herself constantly besought our Lady, under her title of the Faithful Virgin. An old scholar of La Charité solicited the admission of an orphan, whose case was a particularly interesting one; but the poverty of the community compelled them to refuse. Touched with compassion, Henriette made a vow to the Faithful Virgin to take the child as one of her orphans, if that good Mother provided a home in which to receive her. On the 27th of January, 1830, Mademoiselle d'Hendecourt was clothed along with two other young persons from the neighbourhood of Gavrus, who intended to follow Mother St. Mary to La Delivrande. The health of the latter again failed under the pressure of anxiety and grief, and the Superior then consulted the physician at Paris who for years had treated Mademoiselle d'Osseville. He recommended nothing more than sea-bathing, and it was agreed that she should again have this at the proper season.

Meantime Count d'Osseville was straining every nerve to procure a fitting residence, and resolved on purchasing an old dwelling opposite the mission house, though a high price was asked, and he would be obliged to build. The arrangements which he intended carrying out required that he should get possession of a public road, separating the property from the chapel, and for this the authorities threatened to charge its weight in gold. In this matter he went to consult M. Boule, a magistrate, and at that time proprietor of the grounds on which the convent now stands. The old man was very much attached to this property, and took pride in showing it to strangers. Whilst conducting M. d'Osseville and Father Saulet over it, he remarked, 'Sir, what you want is just such a property as this.' 'Exactly,' replied the others; 'but you have no intention of selling?' He admitted that he had not, but added that if he had a good offer, and if his wife and daughter agreed, he would make the sacrifice. It was decided that they should be consulted, and that Father Saulet was to call the next day for a final answer. The previous condition of receiving a good offer was repeated, and Father Saulet begged them to name a sum. On Friday, then, Father Saulet, after fervent prayer to our Lady that he might obtain a favourable decision, went to the house and found the family assembled in discussion of the whole affair. At first they demanded 66,000 francs, though it was evident that 60,000 francs would not be refused, and in the end this amount was offered and accepted, the bargain being concluded on the following day, Saturday.

Some difficulty, however, arose about the terms of payment, and it was proposed to delay the final settlement until the afternoon. This Father Saulet, foreseeing what actually did happen, strenuously opposed, and declared he could not remain to so late an hour. Thereupon, taking the pen, he wrote out a duplicate copy of the conveyance, which was signed by both parties, and delivered to the Count. Not till that moment did M. Boulé realize the fact that, the money once paid, he was bound to vacate the property to which he had so strong an attachment. He tried to raise difficulties, and even wanted to destroy the deed of conveyance; but it was too late, Father Saulet had already presented it at the feet of the Blessed Virgin, thanking her for her protection, and confiding the future well-being of the undertaking still more earnestly to her. In his joy and gratitude the Count charged Father Saulet to announce to his daughter that at last all obstacles were removed. This, however, by no means proved to be the case, for, as Father Saulet remarked, God's works are not usually accomplished without many strokes of the cross. Mother St. Mary, with the utmost delicacy and consideration, informed the Mother Superior of what had been done, and the latter expressed her satisfaction with a step which would tend to the glory of God, although she deeply regretted losing her so soon. She then announced to the community that Mother St. Mary was not to remain at Bayeux.

But God had in store a fresh cause of perplexity for His servant. She received a letter from the Bishop of the diocese, in which he signified to her that, notwithstanding the purchase made at La Delivrande, she must not think of leaving Bayeux until she had secured ten professed Sisters to accompany her, or, at all events, not within two years from the date of his letter. Her first thought was to demand a personal interview with his Lordship, that she might lay before him all the difficulties and trials of her position; but fearing that he had been influenced by one much opposed to the foundation, and was not likely to change, she resolved to suffer in silence rather than wound charity. She wrote to Father Saulet, who was most anxious to remove his spiritual child from her very painful position, and when he recollected the doctor's order about sea-bathing, he became so determined to have it carried out, that the many obstacles raised were immediately put aside. Before going to La Delivrande, Mother St. Mary sent to Paris for the little orphan who had been the object of her vow. As the child happened to arrive at a moment when Father Saulet was in the Convent of La Charité, Mother St. Mary presented her to him, and they together offered her to the Blessed Virgin, before one of the statues, changing her name from Valentine to Mary. This was one drop of consolation in Mother St. Mary's cup, sent to cheer the heart of the future mother of the poor orphans.

The bathing season had at last arrived, and Mother St. Mary set out on July 17, 1830, for La Delivrande, accompanied by her little orphan. After paying her devotions to our Blessed Lady, she visited her future convent, where she was joined by Father Saulet. Together they went over the property in detail, and then returned to offer up a *Te Deum* before the altar. She could not as yet establish enclosure, but she erected a grating in one of the parlours, in order to be able to receive any strangers who might wish to speak with her. Her aunt, the Countess de Valori, whose only daughter had died suddenly a little before, lost her husband about the 30th of July, and came to spend a few days with her niece. When her first grief was abated, Madame de Valori began to consider what her future course of life was to be, and in consulting Father Saulet, her spiritual guide for many years, she found that he had always expected she would consecrate herself to God as soon as the earthly ties which bound her were broken. This reply coinciding with her own earnest desire, she now prepared to arrange her affairs with a view to joining her niece.

A new source of anxiety arose in the events then darkening the political horizon. The Revolution of 1830 had driven the Bourbons from the throne, and Count d'Osseville, true to his principles of patriotism and loyalty, resigned his office. This step considerably diminished his fortune, and he found himself obliged to tell his daughter that the work of La Delivrande must either be immediately organized or entirely abandoned, as he could no longer support both himself and her spiritual daughters at the Convent of La Charité, besides paying for the newly-purchased house.

It was therefore agreed that the Countess d'Osseville should go to Bayeux and lay before the Bishop the urgent necessity of commencing at once the work which he had already sanctioned. The Bishop's reply was that under present circumstances he had forbidden any religious professions in his diocese, and could only permit Mother St. Mary to remain indefinitely at La Delivrande, and there receive such subjects as might come to her, without however giving the habit or receiving vows. This was the only concession that could then be obtained, and trusting that she had at least done something for her daughter's repose of mind, she proceeded to Rouen, where her father's death rendered her presence necessary. The Count was also called to Paris on business, and Mother St. Mary was left with her aunt at La Delivrande under the guidance of Father Saulet, feeling for a short time like a sailor escaped into port from a storm. The calm was but of short duration. The Bishop suddenly ordered her to return to Bayeux and finish her noviceship. On hearing of this new difficulty, her father hastened from Paris to Bayeux, and inquired the cause of the unexpected change. He did not conceal his surprise and displeasure, but declared himself firmly resolved that the foundation at La Delivrande should be effected without delay, or else that he would use all the influence that authority and affection gave him over his daughter, to induce her to leave that particular diocese, concluding with the words: 'Henriette will *never* be a religious at the House of La Charité, as it appears is so much desired. Such is her irrevocable determination, for she has no vocation to it. I will return to-morrow to learn what decision has been come to.'

Next day he found everything changed. The Bishop addressing him said: 'Let Mother St. Mary return for three months to Bayeux, at the expiration of that time she shall take her vows, and I give my word as a Bishop that the following day she shall leave Bayeux for her foundation.' The Count with difficulty acquiesced in this proposal, and returned to tell his daughter the result of the conference. They agreed that, to prove her submission to the orders of the Bishop, she should return the day following to Bayeux, taking only twenty-four hours to arrange matters with Madame de Valori, whom she left in charge of her two little orphans and three subjects destined to be nuns in the future convent. With a heavy heart the poor Mother again left her little community, strengthened by Father Saulet's blessing, who said sadly: 'Go, my daughter, since God wills it so.' We may well imagine how earnestly she recommended her little flock to Mary, as she passed by her sanctuary. On the evening of her return she received a letter from the Bishop strictly forbidding her all communication with Father Saulet even by letter, and telling her that a copy of the letter he then wrote had been sent to Father Saulet with the recommendation that he should come as rarely as possible to Bayeux while she was there. He added, moreover, that all private communication with her future religious was also interdicted, and he once more subjected all her correspondence to the control of the Mother Superior of La Charité. This fresh blow completely stunned the poor novice. At first her strict isolation seemed to weigh her to the earth, but her courage and strength of faith soon restored her confidence, and she determined to suffer all, secure in the protection of her Faithful Mother and Heavenly Father. It so happened that a retreat given to the nuns by Father Madeleine, one of the "Missionnaires de France," ended on that very day. Father Madeleine visited La Delivrande some time before, in order to see Mother St. Mary, but had not succeeded. Father Saulet had since communicated to him some of the difficulties of her position, and had earnestly recommended her to his care. It was providential that he now asked to see her in the parlour, for from that day he was as a guardian angel to her, helping and encouraging her by a thousand proofs of paternal solicitude.

Although the year of Mother St. Mary's noviceship expired on November 27, 1830, political changes were adduced as a reason why she could not be permitted to take her vows, while a still greater difficulty lay in the opposition of the Bishop, whose sincere esteem and affection for her made him the more anxious to attach her to his favourite Convent of Bayeux. He endeavoured by every possible means to shake her resolution, but finding her immoveable he at last gave a verbal consent to the foundation, and fixed the ceremony of the profession for January 5, 1831. Mother St. Mary should have spent ten days in solitude and retirement previously to pronouncing her vows, but this was denied her, and in spite of promises made, first one difficulty and then another was raised. Yet with each trial God granted some special relief. Singularly enough, the Mother Superior invited Father Saulet to preach the retreat of five days for two other Sisters who were to take their vows on the same day as Mother St. Mary. He readily acceded, knowing that he would thus have full authority to see his spiritual daughter, and arrange with her the line of conduct she should follow. He had a long and serious conversation with the Mother Superior, and was both surprised and grieved to hear her retract her solemn promise, given three months before, that the Foundress of La Delivrande should be allowed to leave Bayeux the day after her profession. He indignantly protested against this, and the Mother Superior, finding him inflexible on that point, contented herself with entreating that she should remain till after the elections, which were to take place two months later, solemnly promising that then no opposition to her departure should be made. Father Saulet retired without giving a positive answer as he wished to consult Mother St. Mary herself; she, as may well be supposed, had difficulty in giving her consent, and asked for a night's reflection. The next day, the one preceding her profession, she returned to Father Saulet and said: 'Father, my sacrifice is made: God asks me to suffer two months longer delay,' 'My child,' said the Father much moved, 'I desired it for the good of this community, but I had not the courage to ask it of you.' Nor was this the only point on which she felt anxious, as the pressure put upon her was so great, that up to the very day itself she was uncertain whether her profession would take place or not. The following protestation, the original of which is still preserved in the archives of the Institute, testifies to the coercion which she felt was laid upon her, and to the exact sense in which she made her vows.

In the name of the Father, and of the Son, and of the Holy Ghost. Amen.
I take God to witness.-

1. That employing the same form of vows as the religious of La Charité of Bayeux, I do not mean to contract the same obligations towards that house.

2. That I by no means bind myself to remain in that house, nor to return to it, in case the house at La Delivrande should not exist. That it is through obedience I remain there until March 1, 1831, and that on that day I hold myself free to go to La Delivrande.

3. That while taking the vows according to the Constitutions of the Convent of Our Lady of Charity at Bayeux, yet even if no foundation at La Delivrande is effected, I reserve to myself the right of laying before the Bishop all I feel with regard to my vocation for another community, determined, however, to abide by the decision at which he may in conscience arrive.

Signed MOTHER DE STE.MARIE, novice, born Henriette le Forestier d'Osseville.

Written and signed before my Crucifix, Our Lady of Charity at Bayeux, January 4, 1831.

When the important moment had at last come, and the sermon that seemed too long to her earnest desire was finished, she advanced with rapid step to pronounce those vows which she had so ardently longed to utter. With a voice clear and firm, though betraying her emotion, she pronounced her vows of poverty, chastity, and obedience, and the education of orphans according to the constitutions and for the charity of the orphans of Mary at La Delivrande. 'What does she say?' asked the Prelate in a whisper of surprise, 'My Lord,' said Father Saulet, aloud and gravely, 'she makes her vows for La Delivrande.'

Nor did her trials cease with the profession; new difficulties were continually created, partly from the wish of the Mother Superior of Bayeux to make La Delivrande dependent on Bayeux. She could not bear to see the young Foundress assert the independence of her future community, which however it was essential to preserve.

On the 18th of February, Madame de Valori, who had been compelled by the bishop to come to Bayeux in the preceding month, took the religious habit under the name of Mother St. Anne of the Passion; and one of the subjects from Gavrus was clothed at the same time. On the 23rd , Mother Ste. Dosithée was re-elected Superior of La Charité. Though the house did not then include the twelve professed nuns required by the constitutions, Mother St. Mary was not admitted to take any part in the elections, a fact which proves that the religious did not consider her as any longer a member of the community.

At last the time fixed by the Bishop for her departure arrived, and being now fully convinced of the will of God, he formally established the community of La Delivrande, naming Mother St. Mary its Superior for three years. It was arranged that she should leave Bayeux on the evening of the 25th of February, travelling after dark, in order not to attract attention to her religious habit, in the then agitated state of the country. Two of the subjects of La Delivrande were provisionally detained at Bayeux, while the latter house lent two religious for a time to fill the offices of Assistant and Zelatrix in the new convent. The separation was very painful to the novices, but they accepted it for the general good.

Chapter VII

Departure from Bayeux. First events at La Delivrande. Visitation of the Cholera.

At four o'clock on the evening of the 25th of February, Mother St. Mary, with the Superior of Bayeux, Mother St. Anne of the Passion, and Count d'Osseville, who, besides writing to the Prefect, had secured the protection of the police, left Bayeux in one carriage; while a second, leaving an hour later, to attract less notice, contained two professed nuns of La Charité, two novices of La Delivrande , and Madame de Thouri, the mother of the Superior of Bayeux, who wished to make the journey with them.

'We arrived at Caen,' writes one of the party, 'at about seven or eight in the evening and went to the hospital of St. Louis, where we were expected and received by Father Paysan (afterwards Bishop of Angers) and Madame de Montpinson (cousin of Mother St. Mary and a religious at the Hospital of St. Louis). Wearing our long black choir cloaks, we were taken into the community room, where the religious were assembled. After kneeling to receive the blessing of the Mother Superior we conversed with the nuns until the arrival of the other carriage, when we went to supper. After which our Mother had an interview with Father Paysan, who impressed on her the importance of maintaining the independence of La Delivrande.

'The next morning, between seven and eight o'clock, we were at the door of the beloved Sanctuary of La Delivrande. We went into the sacristy and waited for Father Saulet, who had gone to the convent, not thinking that we should venture to stay at the chapel. He speedily arrived, and we knelt to receive his blessing given with the profound emotion that he must have felt at seeing his hopes realized after so many vicissitudes. We entered the chapel in procession, genuflecting two and two before the Blessed Sacrament, and then knelt with happy hearts round her who was especially our Mother. Wrapt in our own thoughts we did not perceive that a crowd of curious visitors were stealing into the chapel, and when, on hearing the little bell announcing the beginning of Mass, our Mother slightly moved towards the altar, amongst those who pressed around she recognized her two little orphans of La Delivrande.'

Earnestly and ardently in their communion did they promise God, through the Holy Virgin, that the institution which they were the first to represent should ever be distinguished by its fervour and regularity, its obedience and love of poverty; that its riches should consist in the number of its orphans, and the love of humiliation be its daily bread. They must, however, leave the chapel with its miraculous statue, which they little expected ever to see again. When they reached their new home they found Father Saulet and Count d'Oseeville waiting to receive them, and again knelt to obtain the father's blessing as their Superior. After visiting the house and gardens, the enclosure was put up, each nun was installed in her office, and the lay sisters began to cook the dinner. Hampers and boxes were soon unpacked, and the refectory was prepared, the two best rooms on the ground-floor having been already set apart for the chapel. Their community room had to do duty as novitiate, chapter room, linen room and sacristy. The community, exclusive of the lay-sister, numbered six persons when the door of enclosure was fastened and the keys handed by Father Saulet to Mother St. Mary, who the same evening gave her first benediction to her daughters. The next morning High Mass was sung, and during the *Te Deum* which followed each religious came and kissed her hand, acknowledging her as her Superior. The Blessed sacrament was exposed all day, the religious relieving each other in adoration, so that our Lord was never left alone.

Mother St. Mary, after all her trials, felt that peace and joy which comes only after the patient endurance of much suffering. She sometimes asked Father Saulet with a smile if she was really at La Delivrande. 'My child,' he answered , 'I too think I must be dreaming.' Within a day or two Father Saulet was canonically appointed Superior, and from this time he fulfilled with equal skill and devotedness not only the office of superior but that of confessor, conferred on him by the Bishop. Every morning after his Mass at the convent, Mother St. Mary gave him an account of all that had passed during the preceding day, when his advice and instruction gradually trained her in the care of souls and the practice of perfection, while his weekly conferences and private directions helped to develop the spiritual growth of the other members of the Institute.

We need not here enter into any details of the care and affection bestowed by Mother Ste. Mary upon her daughters; instances will occur in the course of the following pages, and will suffice to show the spirit which animated her. It was truly edifying to see how Mother St. Anne, who, as Madame de Valori had undertaken the part of counsellor and guide, now submitted herself to her niece's government with all the docility of a child. In this obedience she took for her motto the word 'To forget all, to be ignorant of all, to deny oneself in all.' Her example exercised a happy influence over the younger sisters. Mother St. Mary on her side knew how to mingle respect with authority in her consideration for her venerable aunt who had been her friend and support during all past trials. She neither allowed her private feelings to mitigate the rule, nor the rule to weigh too heavily on the advancing years of one who, for long after this, still continued to be a model of regularity.

Although new postulants arrived daily, and the foundress rejoiced to mark the spirit of poverty and mortification and of active obedience to herself which pervaded the novitiate, yet her views for the adoption of orphans were still thwarted. Preferring obedience to all other virtues, she resolved to abide God's good time, and to act upon the maxim which she often repeated to her daughters, 'In listening even to an angel, I may be led astray; but in following obedience, never.'

The grounds of the convent were large, but the house itself was too small to accommodate their numbers; it therefore early became necessary to build. A laundry was most needed, and just then the Abbé de St. Manvieu, though totally unknown to the house, sent the amount required. On another occasion when money was much wanted , the religious applied with confidence to their Faithful Mother, and in a few hours one of their number, who had a sum placed in the foreign stocks, received a letter from her agent announcing an unhoped-for dividend and enclosing 3,000 francs. Count d'Osseville also, not content with what he had already paid, advanced to Mother St. Mary the share in his property which would ultimately come to her, and this enabled them at once to begin building a chapel. The plans were prepared, and the work was in great part superintended by the Mother Superior herself. The chapel once finished, other buildings were commenced; an establishment for the orthopaedic treatment was opened, and the Superior's personal experience and motherly care, aided by a skilful medical attendant from Caen, soon attracted patients. The number of orphans began rapidly to increase, and the arrival of new postulants soon formed a well-filled novitiate. Mother St. Antony (Mdlle. d'Hendecourt) having been professed at Bayeux, replaced as Assistant Mother St. Alphonsus, who was recalled to her own convent; and on the 19th of March, 1832, Mother St. Anne was the first to take her vows at La Delivrande. On her appointment to the office of Zelatrix (connected with such external points as provisions and the general order and cleanliness of the house), the last member of the Bayeux community left them, so that Mother St. Mary then had the happiness of seeing herself surrounded by all her children, and her convent placed in a normal and independent position. To be able to carry on so many different works at the early age of twenty eight, after a short and disturbed noviceship and with her very delicate constitution, Mother St. Mary must have united to her great graces an inexhaustible mental and bodily activity, directed with much prudence and method. Though suffering great pain and fatigue at the same time, she was never observed to despond or give herself any ease, nor even to allow a shadow to pass over the natural gaiety of her disposition.

But the zeal and charity of the young Foundress were now called forth in quite another direction. The cholera had already spread its ravages through several parts of France, and as medical skill seemed powerless to arrest its advance, the dearest friends of the stricken were too terrified to remain beside them. Mother St. Mary's kind heart was deeply touched, and she asked permission to make a vow, that if the cholera appeared at La Delivrande, she would go out of the convent and tend the sick, and in this her daughters eagerly begged they might unite with her. Father Saulet consented, and came at three o'clock on Good Friday to receive their vow. That of the novices was made dependent on their parent's consent. Mother St. Mary seized the occasion of a visit of the Bishop to obtain from him the authorization necessary for its execution. Much moved by the demand, he very heartily granted it, and God soon called on them for its fulfilment.

On the 26th of July the first distribution of prizes to the orphans took place. The Countess d'Osseville, always on the look-out for some means of affording pleasure to her daughter, provided the prizes, and received in return that which she had despaired of ever possessing, a likeness of Mother St. Mary surrounded by her five little orphans. It was Father Saulet, who with thoughtful delicacy, had arranged this surprise for one whom both the religious and the children called with affection 'Our Mother d' Osseville.' He had succeeded in overcoming the repugnance of the humble Foundress, in whose eyes a desire expressed by her Superior amounted to an order. The very next day a note from Father Saulet informed them that several people in La Delivrande had been seized with the cholera, adding that he would come in a few minutes to take some of the religious to attend the sick. All were eager to go, but at once acquiesced when Mother St. Mary named herself and three others as those who were to begin this work, and these, having taken the requisite precautions, held themselves in readiness. Father Saulet on arriving assured them that whether they returned unharmed to the convent, or fell victims to the disease, he should equally regard them as martyrs of charity. In silence, with their veils down, they went first to the miraculous statue and recommended themselves to Mary. The villagers regarded them with surprise and admiration as they passed along, and hushed the noise made by the children. Mother St. Mary then placed her daughters in the houses most in want of succour, addressed some words of encouragement to the sick, and returned with the portress to the convent, where she found the orphans in loud lamentation, persuaded they would never see the good nuns again. She calmed them with a gentle reproof and an appeal to their faith.

The pestilence continued to make rapid progress, and it was soon hardly possible to bury the members struck down in a few short hours. Such was the terror that the inhabitants fled to the neighbouring villages, where, being refused admittance, they were obliged to put up tents in the open country. At first two nuns always went together, but this rule had soon to be abandoned, as each one had six or seven patients to take charge of. When a sick person died, the religious who was attending went to look for the nearest Sister, that together they might render the last offices, before they hastened to soften the terrors of death to some other patient. Fearing lest the nuns might sink under these heavy duties, Mother St. Mary arranged that they should relieve each other day and night; and in spite of all the extra work thrown on them, none of the community exercises were interrupted. Father Saulet himself was attacked, and highly would they, like the daughters of St. Francis of Sales, have esteemed the favour of being allowed to attend on their spiritual Father; but circumstances rendered this impossible. In this great trouble Providence sent them as Director Father Ronsin, a Jesuit, whom political events had obliged to take refuge for a time at La Delivrande. Mother St. Mary stood in need of help, for other trials besides fatigue were pressing upon her. Her zeal was criticized and her intentions misinterpreted by those who should have been the first to support her. God often permits that the greatest trial of those whom He loves should be disapproval expressed by the good. In answer to the Reverend Mother's complaints, Father Ronsin replied: 'But, my daughter, do you not see that Divine Providence is just now occupied in building up your house in spiritual as well as in temporal strength? If you met with nothing but praise and approbation, would you not all be exposed to pride? God will provide. He keeps an account of all that you do for Him, whilst He shields your growing virtue from great danger.'

Fr. Saulet recovered from his attack of cholera, but the disease spread, and almost filled the whole neighbourhood with the dead or the dying, and every nun who was able to pass the night out of the convent was engaged at the beside of some afflicted patient. The horrors of these death-bed scenes were one night aggravated by a furious thunder-storm, which set on fire some buildings in the village, adding to the general consternation. Even such scenes were not without their amusing and comic side. Thus some, whose friends the good nuns assisted, made an ostentatious display of their anxiety lest the Sisters should be lifted up by flattery; and in one or two instances, the very persons who had with the utmost haste deserted their parents, brothers, or sisters, ran back to their shops to ask the nun to sell for them as usual, and to be sure not to let anything go too cheap. The cholera spared all the inmates of the convent; but a man who worked for them, and whose cottage stood against the outer wall, was attacked, and the religious in this case attended him.

Up to the middle of August the scourge continued its ravages with even increasing intensity. In this distress all eyes turned to the Blessed Virgin, and a general request was made that the miraculous statue should be carried in solemn procession through the streets of La Delivrande, in order that God's anger might be turned aside through her intercession. The Bishop gave permission, and named the feast of the Assumption as the day for the procession. This news inspired courage in the terrified inhabitants, for they returned at once to the village and hastily prepared decorations and altars of repose on which to place the statue which they so greatly venerated. More than a thousand men, together with a large number of women, took part in the procession. The religious were specially authorized to attend, and were headed by Fr. Saulet reciting the Rosary. At the hour fixed a body of ecclesiastics advanced through the streets, bearing the statue on a raised platform. The religious received it from them, and afterwards delivered it to a confraternity of men, who in their turn were succeeded by young girls in white, and thus it was carried within the enclosure of the convent, where a beautiful altar of repose had been prepared. Mother St. Mary playfully threatened that she would beg our Lady not to allow herself to be taken back to her own chapel; but Fr. Saulet in some fear lest it might possibly be granted, strictly forbade her to make such a request. The utmost piety and order had reigned during the ceremony . The simple villagers sobbed aloud, and earnestly cried: 'Mary, you are our Mother, our only help; Oh, good Mother, cure us.' The sick were laid at the doors of their houses, and invoked her as her image passed, while the men, in earnest and sonorous voices, chanted *Salus Infirmorum ora pro nobis.* The crowd became so great that the Benediction of the Most Holy Sacrament was given from an altar erected at one end of the public square, when the people were congregated together paying. Their confidence was rewarded; the protection of Mary was speedily manifested, for no fresh attack occurred, nor did any of the sick afterwards die.

The religious returned to the peace of their enclosure filled with gratitude to the Faithful Virgin for having so wonderfully protected them, and in thanksgiving for this great favour, Mother St. Mary promised to receive as many of the children left orphans by the scourge as should be offered to them. A considerable number were thus admitted.

Notwithstanding all these external responsibilities and distractions , the Reverend Mother never neglected to watch over the spiritual advancement of her religious, and at her desire a retreat was preached to them by the Rev. Father Saulet as a preparation for the renewal of their vows. Meantime the building of the chapel went forward, and on the 4th of October, 1832, the Bishop arrived to bless it. He expressed his sorrow for all the suffering which he had previously inflicted on Mother St. Mary before her profession, and frequently said to the nuns, when they came around him on his visits: 'Oh, if you only knew, my dear children, how much I made your poor Mother suffer at Bayeux.' He was more than ordinarily kind on this occasion, and testified his heartfelt satisfaction at the flourishing state of the community.

Chapter VIII

Illness of Mother St. Mary. Her miraculous cure. Mother St. Mary's own narrative.

The month of Mary had always been a season of graces and favours for her children at La Delivrande, but it was peculiarly so in the year 1833, as we shall see.

For sometime Mother St. Mary's health had been failing, when on the 7th of May she was attacked with what did not at first seem to be alarming symptoms, but as these became greatly aggravated in a few hours , an express was sent off to Caen at night for the doctor. He could not come till the next morning, by which time the malady had assumed so alarming a character that little hope of recovery was left. Father Saulet administered Holy Viaticum to her, for her intense sufferings demanded all the succour that could be procured. The community present tried in vain to stifle their sobs at the thought of losing one so justly dear and precious to them, and who humbly asked their pardon for all her past shortcomings. When they withdrew from fear of fatiguing her, they went to plead before the Blessed Sacrament for her life.

Dr. Vatel, finding his remedies ineffectual, requested that the family physician should be sent for, but meanwhile told Father Saulet it was time to give her Extreme Unction, and whilst that Sacrament was being administered, he warned the Father in Latin to make haste. In fact, before he had finished she sank into a fainting fit which continued for a considerable time, until she woke up suddenly as from a sleep, and said in a tone of mingled disappointment and confidence, 'If you want me to get better, you must send all the children to pray before the miraculous statue.' Though the orphans had only just returned from it, Father Saulet directed that they should at once go back, giving permission, however, to the younger ones to remain behind, at the suggestion of the Mother Assistant. Afterwards the latter bitterly regretted this act of mere human prudence, when she marked the very tedious convalescence of the poor Mother, who though rescued from the jaws of death, was for months deprived of the use of her limbs, for she felt convinced that, had she blindly obeyed, a complete restoration would have been granted at once. Mother St. Mary afterwards related in conversation with her daughters that God had revealed to her the certainty of her cure if all the orphans had asked it at the pilgrimage; but that it cost her a great effort to tell this, so that when she heard the Mother Assistant's objection, she inwardly rejoiced in the thought that God had been satisfied with her obedience, and did not require her to come back and resume her cross.

Hardly had the children offered up their fervent petitions to the Faithful Virgin in favour of their beloved Mother, when an unexpected change took place . Her body, which had already assumed the coldness of one in the agony of death, recovered its heat and vitality; her features, which had become livid, returned to their natural colour, and all signs of death speedily disappeared. The community were still rejoicing over this sudden relief to their feelings of intense anxiety, when the Count and Countess arrived with the other doctor. Just as he was getting into the carriage to go with his wife to Gavrus, the Count had heard of the express sent to the doctor. He hurried to him, and seizing the letter read, 'Come quickly, dear friend, Madame de Ste. Marie is at the last extremity, my science is exhausted. Lose not a moment, you will scarcely find her alive.' The Count dragged the doctor with him to the carriage, and springing in directed to the coachman to drive straight to La Delivrande. He endeavoured to prepare the Countess for the terrible news that might be awaiting them. The nature of this she soon guessed, and as she afterwards related, repeatedly looked upwards, expecting to see her daughter's soul taking flight up to Heaven. Arrived at the gate of the convent, their eyes made the inquiry which neither had the courage to utter. The Portress understood the appeal, and cried out, 'She is spared.' A little orphan who arrived that evening received the name of Deo Gratias, and was accepted as a thank-offering. Gratitude towards the Faithful Virgin, who had acquired a new right to this title, made Mother St. Mary and her daughters desirous of raising a shrine in her honour. An old quarry in the grounds was chosen as the site, and each one worked with energy in order to transform a wild unsightly place into a pretty little grotto. Materials were procured, and the Sisters helped Mother St. Mary to build up a rustic altar and recess in shell work, bringing stones, moss and shrubs, and by the feast of the Assumption, which best recalled to their minds the Fidelity of Mary, everything was in readiness for Father Saulet to bless their little grotto.

At this time the Reverend Mother had the pleasure of receiving a postulant who took the title of St. Francis of Sales, and whose eminent virtue, shown in the simplicity of her obedience, was often a source of edification to her Sisters. For instance, when during recreation one day the nuns had been unable to shut the outer door of the anti-chapel, the Superior briefly told her to go and shut the anti-chapel door. To Mother St. Mary's question on her return, she replied with naive simplicity, 'I tried to shut it, and when I found I could not, I said, "Door shut in the name of holy obedience," and it shut directly.' Mdlle. de l'Espinasse, whom Mother St. Mary had long counted among her daughters, at length found means to follow her vocation, and in the month of August joined her whom she had been the first to call Mother, and who gave her a most joyful welcome. Another consolation came to the Reverend Mother in a visit paid to the community by the Archbishop of Paris, Mgr. de Quélen, on the 8th of September. The Sisters were much struck with the earnestness of his devotion to the Faithful Virgin, which detained him for a long time in the grotto, and on leaving it he exclaimed, 'Oh, how full of love she is!' He was received with marked respect and veneration by the villagers, who all seemed greatly impressed with his air of sanctity.

But Mother St. Mary was never long without a cross, and in December, 1834, a spasmodic attack caused fresh alarm and anxiety to her daughters. Father Saulet having obliged her in virtue of obedience to write all that happened to her at this period, we shall merely condense the good Mother's own account.

'In the name of the Father and of the Son and of the Holy Ghost. Amen.

To the greater glory of our Lord Jesus Christ, of Mary the Faithful Virgin, of St. Joseph, and St. Augustine.

In the month of September, 1834, weak health already prevented me from fulfilling many of my duties as Superior. I could hardly go upstairs twice without help. I could no longer meditate in consequence of continual headaches, and my soul seemed as much wanting in vigour as my body. I suddenly felt a desire to make a retreat of three days, and as I had Father Saulet's permission, I made it by myself while he also was in retreat. It seemed almost folly to undertake one in my state of health; but to these reflections our Lord replied that he would make it with me and for me. So my first words on entering were, "Here I am, Lord, for Thou hast called me," and at once He answered me , "And I am also here, for you have called me." The next moment I was in deep recollection. I made an hour's meditation without difficulty, and this continued all the time of the retreat, during which God showed me the advantage of suffering, but so pointedly, that I asked myself what was going to follow. The lesson of my retreat was that God willed I should entirely forget myself, never considering if a thing were agreeable or disagreeable, but only if it was pleasing to Him.'

'Shortly after the retreat I became much afflicted both in body and mind, and having but little virtue, I could not entirely conceal my sufferings, and often disedified the Sisters who were taking care of me by my impatience and irritation. However, our Father reassured me, saying I was not always mistress of myself. After this illness I remained worse than I had been before it. My head was weaker. I could not bear the least noise , nor movement before my eyes, without great pain, nor could I attend to anything either spiritual or temporal, being obliged to remain in bed till eleven or twelve o'clock, and requiring the lightest and choicest food, so that I had to send to Caen for bread, the kind baked here not being light enough.'

'Just then a letter was received from Prince Hohenlohe, who a year before had been asked to pray for another Sister and myself. No answer had as yet come, but he now wrote announcing a novena, to conclude on Saturday, the 6th of January. The community began it, and I joined with them, but could not continue, because I always have had so much repugnance to petitioning for my cure. During the novena I grew worse, and was confined to bed, and though I much desired to make the day of recollection for the anniversary of my profession, I was obliged to give it up at nine o'clock in the morning. Yet even in this state my mind was often occupied with what I should do when I got better. Such recovery I expected to come miraculously, but only after a long time, because of my little courage in bearing pain. While thus unable to attend to the community I perceived things were not going on so well, and especially that there was less attention to holy poverty. A great number of novices and postulants were without guidance through my being Mistress of Novices as well as Superior, and the absence of general supervision opened a door for abuses which, though trifling as yet, might eventually become serious. I reflected anxiously on what could be done, and being convinced it was impossible for me to resign as yet my post of Superior, I felt deeply grieved, and complained to our Lord, telling Him He must either remove me from the charge, or give me the power of fulfilling its duties. Then when I tried to do a little work, and found I could not, I had recourse to prayer, presenting before God and the Faithful Virgin this young Institute, which I had founded at their command.'

'Sister St. Bernard was suddenly moved to go and beg of our Father Superior that a novena might be begun to the Faithful Virgin, and she remarked complainingly to him, "Father, they don't pray in the way they ought, they only say coldly, 'My God, if it be Thy will.' We must say out boldly to our Heavenly Father, '*Thou must* indeed grant this to us.' " She also begged Father Saulet to order me to make it, and to ask for my cure. On hearing the Father say to me, "I wish this," I felt quite changed; my desire to obey gave me the confidence which had hitherto failed me, and in asking to be cured for the glory of God and the good of the house, I set only two conditions –(1) that if cured I might offer myself to Him to bear all the other crosses He chose to send; (2) that I should ask for health simply as long as I was Superior, offering to return afterwards to the state in which I was at that time. The novena was arranged to begin on the 10th of January, 1835, and the Father permitted me to pass the day in retreat if I were able. During meditation I found myself as interiorly recollected as I had been in November. At its conclusion I went to prostrate myself before the Blessed Sacrament, placing myself in spirit at the feet of Mary. She and her Divine Son both seemed deaf to my prayer, but the idea occurred to me of asking St. Joseph and St. Augustine. When I was kneeling before the statue of the former, I felt indescribable sweetness, accompanied by the assurance that I was about to obtain my cure through Mary, from whom this great Saint bade me ask it.

When I went to St. Augustine, I did not experience the same feeling, but was moved to ask him the grace of carrying out my rule to the very letter. From this moment the whole community, as well as myself, were filled with a special devotion towards St. Joseph, and we reproached ourselves that we had hitherto honoured him so little. During this day of retreat I was interiorly urged to cherish great purity of heart, and I felt deep sorrow at seeing what God would had done for me if I had always preserved it, and what I had thus forfeited by my infidelity. I therefore begged Father Saulet to hear my confession every day during the novena, and felt that God now showed me more clearly what He wanted, because my heart was pure.

'Father Saulet thought the best way of winning God's grace and blessing upon us was to begin the regular yearly visit of the house, reforming little abuses and renewing our fervour. Considerable fatigue was thereby occasioned me, yet I was already so much stronger that I could go upstairs repeatedly and remain standing some time, not indeed without inconvenience, but without being the worse for it. I longed to go down to choir in the evening, but when the hour came pain and fatigue obliged me to go to bed. On the two or three last days of the novena I heard the morning bell, and felt very anxious to rise for the meditation, but was still too weak and suffering. The doctor came on Saturday the 17th, and hearing from the Sisters what I had done for some days, he at first blamed my imprudence, but on feeling my pulse he said, "This is the first time I see you without fever." On Sunday, though fatigued by saying Office, I seemed to have regained, my ordinary state of health, but that was all. On the same day the Father Superior allowed the community to pray to St. Augustine that I might be able to follow the whole rule. As for myself, unaware that the Father had forbidden the prayer to be offered up before that day, I had been fervently praying for this favour, but without success. Now, however, that the community prayed, instead of my usual fatigue at that hour, I felt quite rested and went to evening prayer.

'The next morning at four, hearing the interior voice invite me to rise, it was no longer illness that prevented me, but the devil and mere human prudence. After keenly debating the point for an hour , the voice of God spoke so strongly that I rose on the first striking of the clock, and peace and joy filled my soul. It was settled that all the community should fast the next day, January 20, and offer his act for my cure. The evening before, Sister Bernard, in obedience to a movement of grace, asked leave of Father Saulet to abstain from eating anything next day until my cure was effected. He gave permission, but told me to see she did not go too far, and, observing how well I was, he told me to try and fast myself.'

'At one in the morning I awoke, famishing with hunger, and could hardly wait until the Mass at which I was to communicate. But the more hungry I felt, the more did grace tell me to resist, and even to go and chant the

Office . God also required of me to leave off the delicate food which had been judged necessary, and to make use of the common fare. And here began another violent battle. It seemed folly to chant fasting for the first time, and so exhaust myself; still more so to take heavier food on the day when I had first attempted to resume fasting. Still I had Father Superior's permission, and having obtained it I obeyed exactly. The only time in which I did not suffer from voracious hunger was while engaged in choir. The devil made me really suffer excessively from the fast, and suggested reasons against it, as though I was tempting God; but I heard the same inward voice saying, "Be at rest; it is I who am finishing your cure." I succeeded in carrying out each point, and ate like a hungry person without feeling any discomfort afterwards, though God alone knows how much suffering and interior combat it cost me. Yet He required still more of me. My state of health had compelled me to have a fire every morning and evening, and a Sister slept in my room. God now bade me part with all this and sleep in the dormitory, in one of the ordinary beds and without having a fire. I acknowledge my cowardice and the violence of the struggle that went on within me during five hours before I overcame myself. On my consulting Father Saulet and describing all the difficulty which I felt, he hesitated at first in consideration of my past weak health, but quickly replied "Go, my child; God wills it."

'At dinner-time Sister St. Bernard came up to me and said, "Mother, can I now eat; is your cure complete?" I answered , " My child, I have fasted, I have sung in the choir; I am going to eat the same food as the rest. Is not that enough?" She asked, "And your cell too?" Feeling at last that God did really require this, I sent her to dinner. When night came, the thought of Jesus, my Spouse, in His poverty gave me the needful strength for this last sacrifice. Humanly speaking, each of these acts would have been imprudent, but when once performed I was not affected by them. This was not the case if others tried to make me do what God did not require. Thus Sister St. Bernard, in her excess of zeal, asked our Father Superior to forbid me the use of a foot-warmer at church and in the refectory. I thought that God would later on require me to deny myself this, but that the time had not yet come. Still, as the Superior approved, the next day I did without it, though feeling a reluctance which I quickly stifled, because holy obedience had spoken. But during the night I suffered again very much from accidental circumstances which would have made me suspect the truth of my cure, had not God so positively assured me. I asked Him if I had been faithless in any matter, if He was displeased with me, reminding Him that with the community His glory was implicated in my cure. He gave me interiorly to understand that I had left off thc usc of the foot- warmer before He bade me do so, and had ceased to follow His directions step by step. I promised Him to tell Father Superior and resume it as soon as he permitted. My painful feelings at once disappeared; but this change caused me much humiliation, as I thought the Sisters would lay it down to my softness and self indulgence. Moreover, our Lord required of me to tell Sister St. Bernard herself to get me a fire, which I did as soon as Father Superior gave leave, and so enabled me to act under obedience.

'One would suppose that all this goodness of God to me would have made me very generous. But this it did not do. I had suffered so much in these various interior struggles, that I was almost angry with God for curing me. I could refuse Him anything; but yet I almost reproached Him for giving me so many directions.

'The weakness of my spine as yet prevented my dressing alone, or remaining long in a standing or kneeling position, so I said to our Lord, "Thou seest what remains to be done, Thou must strengthen me if I am to do everything." He replied, "I will not strengthen you, but I will make you straight." I replied almost sharply, "But I do not ask for that; I desire only to dress myself alone." The answer that came to me was, I desire to work a striking miracle," and at these words my heart was inundated with sweetness and consolation. Dinner-time being come, I went to the refectory, and our Lord showed me that henceforth I must drink water, which I have always much disliked. I resolved with some reluctance to ask permission, for I felt that God intended me always to sanctify by obedience what He told me to do. Having obtained permission, for two or three days, I persevered, notwithstanding the physical pain I suffered; and the devil, finding that I stood firm, removed the difficulty.

'Father Saulet decided that we should begin another novena to obtain the further cure and strengthening of my spine, and the Sisters joined in it with great fervour, each one anxious to offer up many acts of mortification for me; but after a few days God made it known that we were retarding the work by too much effort and excitement.

'13 Feb. as the novena produced no results, the spiritual Father deferred it until the 8th of February, the feast of the Most Pure Heart of Mary, and during this interval I was subjected to violent temptations against faith. On Saturday the 7th everithing was a burden to me, especially the idea of the coming novena. I would have given anything to be let alone. On the day of the feast I felt myself urged to remain longer kneeling and standing, and to do without my foot-warmer in the chapel. The Blessed Sacrament being exposed, I remained kneeling or standing during almost all the long Offices, but as before I did all with very great repugnance. I had not the courage to resist our Lord, nor would I yield to Him generously. I could not tear myself from the church, and yet would not ask Him to cure me. I told the Father Superior, who scolded me well for my lack of the spirit of oblation and obedience; so on leaving him I went and asked God's pardon, repeating the same the next day at confession, and God in His goodness pardoned and strengthened me once more.

'Each day our Lord demanded little sacrifices, which to my mortification seemed great, but being faithful enough to render them, He rewarded me by great peace and consolation, yet I felt terrified at the thought of how far He would make me go. On the Wednesday, St. Joseph's Day, whom since my cure I had specially honoured, I felt myself impelled to erect, in act of thanksgiving, a little chapel to his honour, and resolved to beg alms for this purpose. During this week we passed a night before the Blessed Sacrament, relieving each other every hour. When my turn came, which was from twelve till one, I felt no special consolation but yet great peace. I asked God to make my back straight since He had promised this cure, consulting Him as to whether there was any other sacrifice that He required of me. I felt that He was now satisfied, but that the time had not even yet come. After Holy Communion the following day it seemed to me that God would perhaps make me wait several years, but that my trust in Him must not be shaken.'

Mother St. Mary's narrative concludes at this point, and as many of her papers have been destroyed, and those who knew her best died before she did, we have few personal records left. We may, however, so far supplement this narrative, as to state that for a time the Reverend Mother was almost, if not entirely cured, according to God's promise, but that after a few months she fell back again into her former condition of debility. When the narrative from which we have quoted was submitted to Mgr. Quélen, Archbishop of Paris, he expressed himself quite satisfied as to the truth of its statements and its perfect freedom from all exaggeration or self-deception.

Chapter IX

Secular Retreats. Protection of the Convent from fire. Statue of our Lady presented by the Archbishop of Paris.

Mother St. Mary had experienced too much benefit from secular retreats while she was in the world not to wish to procure the same advantage for many other souls. This was one of the original objects of her Institute, and she was determined to carry it out as soon as possible. The first retreat was preached by Father Guyon, a Jesuit, in November, 1835,and about one hundred people took part in it, spending eight days within the convent, in recollection and self-examination, after which they returned to their families, spreading the influence of their example, and promising to come and make another retreat the following year.

The Reverend Mother's health continued good for several months, so that a priest who saw her joining in the regular duties of the day declared that if her cure lasted for three months, it was the greatest miracle he had ever seen.

Being anxious to propagate devotion towards the Faithful Virgin, Mother Ste. Marie petitioned the Bishop that the religious must be permitted to celebrate each year a feast in honour of the Faithful Virgin on the 20th of January, as the anniversary of her miraculous cure. He granted it for one year at first, but repeated the permission in 1836, and afterwards on his death-bed confirmed it in perpetuity. This permission the Sovereign Pontiff ratified in 1854, and extended it to all the houses of the Institute, naming the Mass of the Immaculate Conception as the one to be used on the occasion.

The Bishop, seemingly anxious to give as many proofs as possible of his esteem and affection for the Holy Foundress, came in the course of the following February to receive the vows of Mademoiselle de l'Espinasse, now Mother St. Aloysius Gonzaga, of Mother St. Francis of Sales, and of two other religious, one of whom had been admitted into the orphanage. Two of the Bishop's nieces were received as orphans, though on a different footing from the rest. He visited the orphanage, blessed the children over and over again, and produced an impression not soon forgotten by them. This proved to be his last visit, as he died shortly afterwards..

The second secular retreat took place in June, and was still more numerously attended than the former one had been. At its conclusion, the new chapel to St. Joseph was consecrated by Mgr. Paysant, Vicar General Who celebrated Mass in the little oratory.

About this time the inmates had a narrow escape from fire, caused by the carelessness of the convent servant in not extinguishing the fire of the bakehouse, which was immediately below one of the children's dormitories. The Mother Superior, when aroused, directed that a small wooden statue of Our Lady, the Faithful Virgin, should be carried in to the dormitory, being convinced that she would arrest the progress of the fire. In reward of her faith and confidence the flames were immediately extinguished, the nun who carried the statue found no difficulty in opening several locked doors through which she had to pass, though in her haste she had forgotten to take the key with her. By the time the villagers and Father Saulet appeared on the scene all danger was over. The latter said a Mass of thanksgiving for the community at four o'clock in the morning, and the villagers discussed the event, some in favour both of the good nuns and of our Blessed Lady, others in blame of our Mother St. Mary for having, as they said, irreverently cast the statue of the Blessed Virgin to burn along with the rest. Indeed, considerable opposition was raised, and the question of exaggerated devotion to Mary under the title of the Faithful Virgin was even brought before the Bishop's Council, and a reprimand seemed imminent, when the fact of the miracle granted was considered to be a sufficient answer to all objections. Those whom the Mother Superior herself consulted regarded this event as only a fresh proof of the especial favour with which God rewarded their devotion to the Faithful Virgin, an opinion which was fully justified afterwards in Rome.

As there may still linger in the breasts of some persons a feeling of distrust in the soundness of the special devotion practised to our Blessed Lady in the Institute founded by Mother St. Mary and as some readers may share in that feeling, it will be as well to quote a portion of Father Saulet's lengthened reply to a certain ecclesiastic position, who had written a letter of remonstrance to him on the point.

'You heard, as you believe, from me that the religious at La Delivrande pretend that God can refuse Mary nothing, that they could obtain through her the power of living without eating, or almost without it, and consequently had reduced their allowance each day, until they had impoverished their blood and ruined their health. I ask you to reflect again, for it was certainly not from me that you heard a calumny as false as it is absurd. If the religious had been silly enough to entertain such an idea, I, as Superior, would have had sufficient charity and self-respect to keep it an inviolable secret. The idea of any connection existing between their confidence in our Lady, and their excessive mortification was, I confess, quite new to me till I read your letter. I well remember some excess in their mortifications, by no means an uncommon thing, especially in young and fervent communities, for the line separating what is sound from what is exaggerated or ill judged is not always easily drawn. I may, too, in my anxiety at seeing a few in bad health have remarked to some one, "I think they want to live without eating", but to find more than a joke in such an expression indicates an amount of prejudice against them of which I know your Reverence to be incapable.

'I do not know in what terms the fact mentioned by Mgr. Paysant was presented to you; but, at any rate, it only related to one Sister, who ardently wished that the Reverend Mother's back should be cured. I remember her petition was made to God after the first favour had been obtained, and I do not know if such confidence in our Lord can be taxed with exaggeration.

'I have already addressed to his Lordship a protestation that I attach to the word *Fidelis* no other meaning than that given by the Church, "Faithful to God"; and I am prepared to declare that the religious so understand it, and have thus explained it to their orphans. Mary is the example of fidelity to God at every age and in every circumstance. Moreover, I openly acknowledge that I never blamed them for attaching themselves to the word *Fidelis*, in a secondary if not primary sense, the idea of Mary's fidelity in listening to prayer and obtaining its answer, I have grave authority in my favour. The Jesuit, of whom I spoke to you in reference to M. Le Boucher's work, is of the same opinion, and he even added that God Himself in Sacred Scripture is called "faithful" in the sense *–Fidelis enim Deus qui non...* Yet I did not take the slightest step to obtain his Lordship's authorization. I knew the goodness of his heart, and how much it would have cost him to refuse me.

'SAULET'.

Providence made use of a miraculous occurrence connected with Mgr. de Quélen's visit to the Grotto, to remove the opposition still maintained by a part of the clergy of Bayeux. It appears that the Archbishop on entering the Grotto was penetrated with a special confidence in the Fidelity of Mary, and made a vow that he would himself present a statue in honour of the Faithful Virgin if she obtained a grace which he most ardently desired, viz., the conversion of the well-known Prince de Talleyrand. The Faithful Virgin did not turn a deaf ear to the prayers offered up for him; and his conversion taking place soon after, in the year 1838, the Archbishop prepared to fulfil his promise. A beautiful bronze statue was cast, representing the Blessed Virgin standing on a globe, on which were the words in raised and gilt letters written *Virgo Fidelis*, and beneath them on one side of the globe the inscription, *Congratulamini mihi inveni ovem meam quae perierat, Maii, 17, 1838,* and on the reverse side the words, *Ex voto Hyacinth Ludovici de Quélen Archiepiscopi Parisiensis, pro salute aeterna Principis de Talleyrand ad reconciliationem rite admissi ac perseverantibus paenitientiae signis defuncti. Maii 17, 1838*.

When the Archbishop arrived at La Delivrande on September 7, 1838, Father Saulet informed him of the opposition of some of the clergy to that devotion, of the decision of Rome, and of the impossibility of as yet establishing the Congregation of the Faithful Virgin. 'Perhaps', said he, 'your Grace has been chosen by our Lady to overcome all these obstacles, and to establish the public devotion to her as *Virgo Fidelis*.' Pleased with the idea, the prelate set about the necessary arrangements, having obtained the cordial assent of the Bishop of Bayeux. The statue, nearly four feet in height, was borne in procession by the orphans from the mission house to the pilgrimage chapel, and exposed to the veneration of the people. Then the invocation, *Virgo fidelis, ora pro nobis* having been sung three times, the Archbishop pronounced an eloquent allocution on the Fidelity of Mary. The next day the statue was carried in procession to the convent, and placed on a credence. After the *Sub Tuum*, recited by all present, the Archbishop, Bishop, Vicars-General, and other clergy proceeded to venerate it, and after Vespers, with equal solemnity, it was installed in front of the Grotto, bearing inscribed on its pedestal the many favours already obtained through the intercession of the Faithful Virgin.

How great was the joy and gratitude of Mother St. Mary on hearing those who had been bitterly opposed to her now singing in loud and enthusiastic tones, *Virgo fidelis, ora pro nobis,* the Archbishop having specially demanded that the invocation should be thus repeated; and most complete was the triumph of Mary. In every succeeding visit, Mgr. Robin testified his particular veneration of the Faithful Virgin, saying, 'How much I love that title of the Blessed Virgin!' and once remarking to Mother St. Mary, 'It was she who put the fire out, was it not?'

The Archbishop in particular propagated this devotion to Mary, and a beautiful statue, placed by the religious of Notre Dame (Les Oiseaux) at Paris, above their chief altar, was consecrated by him under the same title. This statue was, so lately as December 8, 1874, crowned by special permission, when also His Holiness attached an indulgence of 300 days to the invocation, *Virgo fidelis, ora pro nobis*. The sacristy of Notre Dame at Paris contains a picture commemorative of the same devotion, the Archbishop being represented as standing before a statue of the Faithful Virgin, made after the design of his own *Ex Voto*.

Such has been the history of the formal adoption of the title of our Lady as *Virgo Fidelis* by the Institute which Mother St. Mary founded.

Chapter X

Illness and absence of Father Saulet. Mother St. Mary re-elected Superior. Accounts of several religious.

The second triennial of Mother St. Mary's government was drawing to a close, and the rule required that another Superior should be elected. More than one voice from without suggested that the Institute was scarcely as yet sufficiently formed, and that in her exceptional position of Foundress, a dispensation from the rule could be easily obtained, but she herself was resolute in laying down her charge. On February 27, 1837, she was canonically superseded, and Mother St. Teresa was elected in her stead, the former receiving the charges of Assistant, Novice Mistress, and Principal Mistress of the orphans. Of these the latter office was especially welcome to her. On the day of the election she led the new Superior into the class-room, saying, 'My children, I bring you my Mother and yours. Love her as I do.' With equal affection and success did she fulfil her charge over the orphans. She was always their mother more than their mistress, and devoted herself to the work of developing their minds and their affections. The humble demeanour of Mother St. Mary and her filial submission to the new Superior elicited the admiration of the orphans. Children are quick observers, and generally form correct judgments. 'After all,' said they, 'she is really her mother, and she is just like her little child. One can see that she rejoices in being no longer Superior, and in making us love Mother St. Teresa.'

A new and unexpected trial soon after fell on the community. Father Saulet had been for some time suffering from an affection of the throat, which rendered complete rest necessary. In the month of January, 1838, he was ordered to pass the rest of the winter in Italy, and to remain there until he was quite cured. The good Superior felt the sacrifice which his absence would occasion to his daughters, especially to Mother St. Mary, and therefore wrote to prepare them gradually for so painful a separation.

During the six months of his sojourn in Italy, letters constantly passed between him and the community at La Delivrande. On one occasion, Mother St. Mary was much distressed at finding no letter addressed to herself, and treating this feeling as a great imperfection, she felt bound to mention it to Father Saulet. His answer certainly shows the watchfulness with which he guarded her against the snare of self-love. He thus wrote: 'I was deeply humbled, my dear daughter, on hearing of the weakness into which you were betrayed by not receiving from me a letter addressed to yourself. I have been directing you for eight years, yet how little have I succeeded in teaching you to die to yourself, to desire that others should receive more honour and respect, that obscurity and neglect should be reserved for your own portion. I feel sure that you repelled this purely human impulse, but your experiencing it at all discloses the imperfection still remaining within, and proves how requisite it is that God should try you, and should root out of your heart all that is opposed to Him. I fear too that you retard my return by being over anxious for it. You must learn to reduce to silence certain promptings of your soul which agitate you interiorly, and in spite of your sincere protestations and sentiments of resignation, prevent you from throwing yourself entirely into the hands of your Divine Spouse, leaving Him free to act, and seeking nothing but His greater glory. What need have you of man if God be for you? Can He not raise up a thousand according to His own Heart? But here I am repeating what I said the other day. Let us *practise*, and we shall be happy.'

A few days after, he again writes.

'At last you shall have a few lines, and a *letter addressed to yourself*, which will, however, impose a fresh sacrifice upon you, as I send it unsealed. It is well that you become accustomed to sacrifices, so as to make them without effort, not as something hard or extraordinary, but as inseparable from your holy state. You must learn to view everything in a spirit of meek and simple piety, which imitates your Divine Master in singleness of heart, and brings you nearer to Him by each sacrifice which you calmly and cheerfully embrace. In a similar way must you regard the real or imaginary trials of others. For yourself, my daughter, go on and fear nothing.' With respect to some particular persons, he remarked: 'They acted in too great hurry and precipitation, —in itself a decided fault. Never forget this, my daughter, but strive to acquire that sweet and abiding union with our Lord, which is not external only and superficial, but is grounded in faith, and draws us to hide in the Heart of Jesus all our personal miseries, all our trials and contradictions, even our scruples of conscience, that we may walk in simplicity and confidence free from every doubt and misgiving, or from darkness and weariness of soul. Be assured that sooner or later God will show you your shortcomings.'

In another letter, dated May 28, 1838, he says::

'I might, perhaps, have scolded you had I been near you when, instead of trusting Jesus, you began to lean upon yourself. But what use would it be to scold you from Rome, when the evil would have been over long before my letter reached you? Try at least to profit by your experience, and remember this is no time for despairing. In spite of all you tell me respecting your interior dispositions, I cannot but detect a want of filial confidence in your dealing with your Heavenly Spouse. You calculate and reason too much. You are too much occupied with what passes in yourself, with what our Lord may think of you, and you are perpetually interrogating Him. Keep your imagination in check, and study to attain singleness of purpose in all you do, without troubling yourself about the results. Your mind would then be much calmer. What is a religious who after eight years of profession gives way to discouragement, notwithstanding all the graces which God has given you? Humble yourself to the earth, be astonished at yourself before God, and assure Him of your regret and resolution to amend. I know how much connection there is between the physical and the moral in your case, but virtue must render the moral superior to the physical, otherwise you will be but a poor religious.'

From Bagnères de Luchon, on his way home, Father Saulet wrote: 'I think my exile has done me good, and I bless God for not having been cured. Ah, His ways are admirable... I do not think you a saint, but I hope you will become one, and I wish much to help you. Go forward in the meantime without examining whence the cross comes. Be careful to humble yourself to nothing before God, having your eyes fixed with confidence and unquestioning trust on Him... Judge of others with all Christian charity... They have good motives that we do not know of. ... Listen to the reproofs addressed to yourself, correct those that are just, and avert those that are unfounded, Let peace, recollection, self-abandonment, and especially humility be your spirit.'

In August, 1838, Father Saulet returned to La Delivrande, to the great joy of the community, and immediately resumed his functions. There had been no real cure of his complaint, but he soon after recovered completely under remarkable circumstances. A religious of La Delivrande offered herself to God to suffer in his stead, and while he recovered his voice she entirely lost hers for several years. After some time, she began to speak a little, though in a very forced and unnatural tone; but her condition remained really unchanged during the rest of her life, which was prolonged beyond that of the Father Superior.

The close of this year was made remarkable by the miraculous cure of Mother St. Aloysius Gonzaga, who was attacked by some fatal malady, but after a novena made in union with Prince de Hohenlohe, she quite suddenly recovered her health and strength. Another mark of God's favour was granted in the case of a blind postulant lately admitted by especial favour. She had lost her sight at the age of four, but was endowed with a wonderful memory and great natural abilities. Under the name of Mother St. Vincent de Paul she speedily realized the hopes that had been entertained of her usefulness and edification. She was soon able to recite the Office in choir, and fulfilled her fourth vow by teaching catechism to the orphans, for which work she was especially qualified. She was appointed to give the signals for the duties of the house, and was also portress, and in this office she showed wonderful dexterity, making her way from one place to another, and giving excellent example to all by her gentleness, piety, and charity. She was profoundly thankful to Almighty God for having deprived her of sight, and thus preserved her from many occasions of offending Him.

On February 26, 1840, Mother St. Mary was unanimously re-elected to the charge of Superior. Father Saulet, on placing in her hands the insignia of office, said: 'I return you, my daughter, the cross that you have already borne during six years, and of which you well know the weight. Remember you are but a useless servant.' Mother St. Mary entered on her charge with the same energy, love of regularity and zeal for the progress of her religious, which had marked her first administration.

About this time the Abbé Achard of St. Manvieu desired to place his orphanage at Blon under the care of religious, and he asked Mother St. Mary to take charge of it. Most willingly the zealous Mother acceded, and the preliminaries were almost arranged, when an unexpected difficulty arose in the proposal that the two houses should have but one Superior, an arrangement not allowed by the constitutions of Bayeux, which, as we have seen, the Reverend Mother had been obliged to adopt. Anxious to extend her charity and develope her Institute, she applied to Mgr. Robin for leave to alter this prohibition, but God's time had not yet come, and as the Bishop refused leave, Mother St. Mary sacrificed her wish to obedience, and could only pray that some devoted soul might be raised up to undertake the work in her place. A favourite maxim with her was this, 'If there is some good work which you cannot yourselves undertake, rejoice when others can do it instead of you, and help them with all your power to advance the glory of God.' The Reverend Mother's prayer was heard, and she learned with joy that the Countess of St. Leonard had undertaken the foundation in which she was to be assisted by Father Madeleine. She wrote in very cordial terms to the Countess, joyfully acceded to her request of being allowed to make her noviceship at La Delivrande, and with open arms received her, along with a postulant, who was intended to be her companion. Madame de St. Leonard wished to found an institution under the name of 'Filles de la Misericorde du Saint Coeur de Marie', to provide for the education of the poor children of the country, for visiting the sick, and giving retreats. As her noviceship was especially directed to prepare her for the office of Foundress, Mother St. Mary generously gave her every opportunity of gaining an insight into religious life, even admitting her into the council and chapter-room. On her taking the religious habit, all the novices were assembled, and their Mother Superior with rare disinterestedness recommended them to weigh well before God which Institute they preferred, adding that she would always be happy to see them engaged in that good work which she was not herself allowed to undertake. In return, Mother du Saint Coeur de Marie afterwards felt the deepest gratitude to the community amongst whom she had been thus received and often said to her daughters, 'My children always be grateful to the religious of La Delivrande, for they did your mother more good than I can tell you.'

As Mother St. Mary was not permitted to assume the charge of more orphans, she gave herself up to her own especial duties with renewed and increasing energy. Although charged with the care of the whole community, she bestowed her personal attention on the forty young girls who were under the orthopaedic treatment, accompanying the doctor every week in his visit to them, that she might from her own observation judge of their improvement. A boarding-school was also opened, to which her maternal affection and sound wisdom soon attracted and attached many pupils.

The secular retreats were every year more numerously attended, as there were then but few houses in which these exercises were given. In 1840 over three hundred and forty persons took part in the retreat at La Delivrande; at other times as many as four hundred have joined in it, and such abundant fruit has resulted that a neighbouring curé begged the Reverend Mother never to refuse even one person, adding: 'May these retreats last as long as your community does.' All the sisters were glad to bear any inconvenience, or to bestow themselves in the most impossible places, in order to contribute to so good a work.

Another great consolation afforded Mother St. Mary in the early part of 1841 was the admission of a young Protestant into the Catholic Church. We are not at liberty to publish the circumstances attending her conversion, but it was on the 20th January, the feast of the Faithful Virgin, that Father Saulet, with the Bishop's authority, received her renunciation of heresy and profession of faith, in the presence of all the community. Meantime God called upon the holy Foundress to surrender into His hands another of her religious. Sister St. Agatha, who had the care of the younger children, the class of the Infant Jesus as it was called, after seven years of untiring self-sacrifice to these little ones fell into a decline. A long illness of several months tried, but could not exhaust, her unwearied patience. During several hours before her death shc remained silent and motionless, as in a trance, when suddenly her features were lighted up with an expression of heavenly joy, and she endeavoured to form some inarticulate words. The next moment her countenance resumed its usual expression, and she quietly expired, leaving on every bystander the impression that her Divine Lord or His holy Mother had certainly appeared to her in a vision.

On February 27, 1843, Mother St. Mary was again re-elected, to the great joy of all her children. It was then that with much care and skill she elaborated the system of education and instruction now employed by her daughters, whom she carefully formed to its use, explaining those principles and methods which were afterwards more completely developed at Norwood.

A large additional building, having the lower part partitioned out in parlours, and the upper stories used for infirmaries, was now constructed. On the last Sunday in May it was blessed by Father Saulet under the title and patronage of St. Sebastian. The house of La Delivrande contained thirty-seven professed choir nuns, fourteen lay-sisters, and four novices. Several reasons rendered Mother St. Mary anxious to have a Sister who could teach English to the boarders, and so, relying much on the excellence and obedience of Mother St. Francis of Sales, of whom we have already spoken, she directed her to make a novena for that intention. It was answered by the unexpected arrival of a young Scotchwoman, whose history was another example of God's wonderful mercy, and of the Providence which can convert the bitterest trials into a source of the greatest happiness.

The young neophyte arrived on March 23, 1844, and was received with a most cordial welcome and cheerful smile. Her every wish was anticipated, every want foreseen by Mother St. Mary, and, speaking to her on the question of providing a sponsor, she made choice of her own father, Count d'Osseville, who ever after continued to show the deepest interest in the young convert. Father Saulet was struck with her thorough knowledge of the Catholic faith and of Holy Scripture. The special gifts which he remarked in her soul led him to admit her into the bosom of the Church at once. Two days after her reception she made her first Holy Communion, and it was not long before her earnest entreaties obtained for her the further grace of admission into the religious life, for on the 5th of May the Father Superior placed on her head the postulant's veil, saying: 'How? Is it you, my dear child? Your brow is still wet with the waters of regeneration which we poured on it but a few weeks ago, and you aspire to walk in the paths of perfection.' Shortly afterwards wearing her baptismal robe and postulant's veil, she received Confirmation, and on the day of her clothing the white robe first worn by her suggested to the preacher an eloquent appeal, in which, after addressing one of the future novices by her side, then clothed in the rich garments of the world, with the words: 'You, my Sister, are about to strip yourself of the garments of vanity, trample them under foot,' he turned to the recent convert, saying: 'But you, my Sister, I would bid to lay aside your robe with respect, kiss it with affection, for it is the symbol of your innocence, preserve it therefore until death.'

But if the religious family of Mother St. Mary was increased by the admission of new members, several were called away from it in rapid succession, to the lively sorrow of the good Foundress. Of this number we mention only one, Mother St. Aloysius, naturally of a very happy and kindly disposition, which made her a general favourite. After a few years spent in the practice of many virtues Mother St. Aloysius, though still comparatively young, had a stroke of apoplexy. Feeling from the first that the attack was likely to be fatal, she expressed her willingness to die. During the three days which intervened, she was literally tortured by the physicians in their endeavours to save her life. In her delirium her mind ever recurred to God. 'Tell me,' she stammered, 'in what language, English, French, or German, I can best tell God I love Him.' In the agony of her pain, she suffered no complaint to escape her lips. When the doctor talked of applying the strongest possible blisters and vesicants, in hopes of producing an irritation which might withdraw the disease from the brain, the poor patient, who had lost the power of speech, turned pale, but yet gave a sign of acquiescence. After submitting to the fresh torture inflicted a slight reaction was the only result. This restored speech to her for a few hours, during which she exclaimed with deep feeling: 'O my God! What a happy nun I have been! What shall I give my Jesus for having called me? Mother, I will pray for you. You have made me so happy.'

On the 14th of August, while the community were chanting the *Te Deum*, on the eve of the Assumption, she calmly expired. For long she had the supervision of the farm-servants and workmen, and their grief at her loss was very sincere. A Sister, who went to see whether the digging of her grave was finished, observed the man's tears falling thickly on the ground as he worked.

In 1845 Father Saulet was called to give a mission in a district where the Revolution has produced bitter fruits. In the readiness and ingenuity of her zeal Mother St. Mary confided the soul of a sinner to each one of her daughters, that by her prayers and other good deeds the grace of repentance might be obtained for it. Each vied with the other in making generous sacrifices. The most remarkable conversions resulted from the mission, which was a real and solid triumph for religion, and God only knows how far the united sacrifices of a few obscure religious may have contributed to this great good.

The second triennial of Mother St. Mary's rule having come to its close, Mother St. Aloysius Gonzaga was elected in her place, and the same filial submission which had marked the good Foundress' manner on her former retirement from office was again repeated. Mother St. Mary became Assistant and Novice-Mistress, a charge which she fulfilled with the utmost care and zeal, devoting all her time, her energies, and the remarkable gifts she had received to the spiritual advancement of her daughters.

The edifying death of Mother St. Francis of Sales, with whom we are already acquainted, took place about this time. We have every reason to believe that, entering early into religion, she brought with her the baptismal robe of innocence unsullied, and retained all its purity till death. It seemed as though her life were shortened by the overflowing consolations which she enjoyed, and that her heart was too small for the ardour which consumed it. During her long malady the Infirmarian had not remarked a single imperfection. Several times when absorbed by the contemplation of God, the Blessed Virgin, and St. Aloysius Gonzaga, her favourite Saint, she exclaimed: 'Oh, how lovely Mary is! I cannot tell you how lovely.' And on the 21th of June she said: 'How beautiful Aloysius is: I could not have believed he was so beautiful. Nothing on earth can express it.' Two hours before her death she begged Father Saulet to sing with her the cantique, *Sainte Cité*, answering to the English hymn, 'O Paradise,' and when her own voice failed, she asked Mother St. Cecilia to continue it, and then gradually sank to rest, leaving behind her a feeling of profound peace.

Chapter XI

Foundation in England proposed. Journey to London. Consent of the Bishop. Arrival at Sydenham Grove.

On February 26, 1848, the anniversary of the foundation, Father Saulet announced to the astonished religious that France was a Republic. Mother Ste.Marie, who had not forgotten the horrors of the first Revolution, was full of anxiety lest her daughters might be constrained to leave the convent, and therefore her thoughts turned towards England as a refuge in case of serious troubles. From that date till the month of June fervent prayers were offered up by the community to obtain the light of the Holy Spirit, that they might know the will of God as to what steps should be taken. Mother Ste.Marie much loved and often used the beautiful prayer, 'O Lord, be in us, and with us, in all our concerns and interests, at all periods, and in all places, in time and eternity, whatsoever it shall please Thee; out of love to Thee we desire whatever thou desirest.'

But well aware of the difficulties attending the enterprize, she begged God to give some indication of His will. For several years the fatigue and confusion occasioned by the secular retreats had invariably caused serious indispositions to several religious.

This time in closing the retreat, which had been especially well attended, she assembled her daughters, and after speaking to them of the probability of a foundation in England, she forbade them to go to the infirmary. All were obedient; not one was attacked with sickness, a circumstance which she read as a sign that God favoured the development of the Institute. Like many others in the same position, it was under the pressure of intense interior trials, very partially known to any one, that she pursued the idea of a new foundation. All she had hitherto done seemed to her useless and unblest, and this through her own fault. She accused herself of pride and presumption in having allowed herself to become the foundress of a new Institute. In the agony of her mind she exclaimed, like her Divine Master, 'My God, my God, why hast Thou forsaken me?' Heaven and earth seemed equally obdurate, since, in order to purify her yet more, God permitted that for a whole month Father Saulet refused to see her, and when at last she obtained an interview of five minutes, the time was spent in discussing an entirely different subject. Her only consolation was to throw herself at the feet of Jesus, and abandon herself wholly to His love and care. No murmur escaped her lips. She suffered for the new foundation, as she had suffered for the first, and retained throughout her confidence that in God's good time her wishes would be executed. She afterwards said in a private conversation with one of her daughters, that Norwood had restored her to life, for if that foundation had not taken place she must have died of her intense mental suffering. Yet when the project was almost decided on more difficulties were before her. Father Saulet would not take upon himself the responsibility of recommending a new foundation in a foreign land, and required her to settle so important a step independently of him. On this she asked a little time for reflection; and having seen before God that the salvation of many souls was to be won by embracing the way of the Cross, by accepting many humiliations and contradictions, her generous heart no longer hesitated, and returning to her director she answered with firmness, 'Yes, Father, I take the responsibility of this foundation on myself.' Then he rejoined, 'You yourself must be its Superior.' She bowed to his will in acceptance of this fresh burden. To complete her sacrifice he added that it was for her to prepare her parents, and obtain their consent to this separation, for he would have nothing to do with it. To this also she consented. The Faithful Virgin supported her while the Father made her advance by so thorny a path , for, as Bishop Grant afterwards remarked, the souls which Father Saulet had formed were all highly tempered, and had been shaped with many a stroke on the anvil of the religious life.

In the same year the medal of the Faithful Virgin was executed for the Institute. The design given to the engraver represented on one side Mary in the Temple, with the words, *Virgin Faithful to God, pray for your children*, and on the reverse side our Lady standing upon clouds, extending her arms to a nun and to an orphan placed at her feet, having beneath the words, *Virgin Faithful to men, watch over your children.* As though guided by some providence the engraver represented the religious and orphan as standing on the shore, while Mary appeared on the opposite side beckoning them over, and the latter design was realized a few months after, when eighteen religious with the Foundress as their head crossed the channel to devote themselves to the care of orphans. Mother St. Mary had always longed to work for foreign missions, and her fervent charity was particularly touched by the forlorn condition of Catholic orphans in a Protestant country.

When it was necessary that active steps should be taken for the foundation, Father Saulet went to Paris to procure information upon the plan. He applied to the most eminent people for an introduction into London, but though all approved and encouraged, none could hold out to him any definite opening. Paris was not yet cleared of the barricades of February, and a general feeling of insecurity still reigned. The good Father was about to return in despair, when the superior of St. Sulpice gave him the name of one of their brethren residing in a suburb of London, and to him Father Saulet immediately wrote. The Rev. M. Quiblier, the priest in question, was at this moment endeavouring to form a small congregation out of the Catholics dispersed around Norwood, whose children were daily being swallowed up by the Protestant workhouses, and he earnestly prayed that God would enable him to find a remedy for this great evil. More than once he had consulted Dr. Wiseman, Vicar-Apostolic of the London District, who fully shared in the pain which he felt. He knew well that the numerous conversions attending his efforts by no means counterbalanced the ravages which the workhouse system was inflicting. He had already provided an asylum for the boys, and was anxiously considering what could be done for the girls. The resources of the Catholics were still more limited then than they are now, and neither he nor Dr. Wiseman could do more than pray and hope. The good priest began a novena to our Lady, and each day at Holy Mass laid before God his ardent desire of seeing an orphanage for girls established, and to this Father Saulet's letter came as an answer.

Often during the days which followed, his favourite pious ejaculation was heard, 'May God be blessed, and we will bless Him, and He will bless us, and we shall be blessed.' A reply was speedily sent to Father Saulet, and after a short correspondence, at Dr. Wiseman's urgent invitation, a visit to England was undertaken by Father Saulet, Mother St. Aloysious Gozanga, then Superior, and Mother St. Mary and Nives. They were most kindly received, and it was settled that a boarding school for young ladies, and an orphanage for girls should be established at Norwood, the latter to be supported by the Catholics of England and by some French benefactors. On their return to La Delivrande active preparations were made for setting on foot the new foundation. The Bishop of Bayeux readily gave his consent , adding permission to make the necessary change in the Rule. On the 9th of September Mother St. Mary was named Superior, the religious who left being however warned that they must not expect her to remain after February, 1849, when the election of a Superior again came round.

The Countess d'Osseville, in the true spirit of sacrifice, gave her full consent to her daughter's departure to England, and her father, through seventy years of age, prepared to accompany her, and marked his visit as usual with acts of beneficence. On the evening of the 10th September Mother St. Mary assembled her daughters for the last time, for they would never again be with her, addressed to them some words of deep faith and affection. Those who remained were to be like Moses on the mountain, their hands always raised to Heaven in prayer, interceding for their Sisters sent to struggle in the land of heresy, whilst the latter were to edify by their piety and virtue, and draw down God's blessing on their labours; so that although separated they would still have but one heart and one soul, and would preserve the tie between them unbroken, as both would be working for the one common end. Then, amidst their stifled sobs, she blessed all present, and tenderly embraced those from whom she was about to be separated. Her last words on leaving the enclosure the following morning were, 'Be women of faith.' She was accompanied by her father, and Mother Ste. Dosithée, who had the happiness of attending on her. The other religious were to meet her at Honfleur the next day. They left the convent on the evening of the 11th September, whilst the orphans, who had been hitherto kept in ignorance of what was going on, became loud in their lamentations.

Travelling then was not so easy nor so frequent as it is now, and to some of the Sisters 'going to England' seemed more than 'a voyage to New Zealand' would have been to many an English woman. The little band was composed of Father Saulet, who went to install his daughters in their new house, the Rev. Father Vesque, who was selected to be their chaplain, eighteen religious, and the Count d'Osseville, now almost blind, who wished to lay the first stone of their new altar. Besides these were three young persons, an orphan from La Delivrande, who it was intended should aid the Sisters, a young convert whom the Mother Superior had previously taken over from England, and who was now returning to obtain the consent of her Protestant family to devote herself to the service of God, and Mademoiselle Xaverine de Jumilhac, Mother St. Mary's niece, who was to be the first pupil in the boarding school.

On reaching Havre they went to the Convent of the Ursulines, where they were received with true religious hospitality. During the night Mother St. Mary had a serious attack, which for some hours much alarmed her daughters, and made them greatly fear that she would be unable to cross in to England next day. After very fervent prayers had been offered up to the Faithful Virgin she grew better, and was able to embark, and it was on the 14th of September, the feast of thc Exaltation of the Holy Cross, that the religious landed at London. Although their appearance caused considerable astonishment amongst the bystanders, yet all moved aside respectfully, and left a passage for them to the carriages which Father Quiblier had prepared to convey them to their new dwelling in Sydenham Grove, Norwood. On their arrival they were somewhat startled to find in how small a house twenty-one persons were expected to find lodging. They soon learnt that even of this small building only half belonged to them, still they had to pack themselves in it, luggage and all, as best they could. The principal room was set apart for their chapel. A wooden table covered with white and blue paper formed the altar, on which stood a wooden cross and two brass candlesticks. And here the Lord of Hosts came to dwell while the community and one or two neighbouring Catholics were crowded together within a space that scarcely left room enough for the celebrant to move in .

The first act of Mother St. Mary and her daughters was to renew fervently the holocaust which they had made of themselves to the service of God, in the persons of his abandoned little ones, and earnestly did they beg

His help and blessing on their work.
After visiting in detail the house that had been hired and furnished for them, the Mother Superior soon perceived that it was too confined to lodge the religious themselves, still less could they open schools, or receive boarders in it.

The whole available space was occupied by tables and benches of the refectory, by the bed and chair of each Sister, and it was impossible to establish enclosure or privacy when there could be no division from the part allotted to strangers. After they had done their best to settle down, some weeks of very painful inaction followed, rendered all the more irksome from its strong contrast to their previous active life. Mother St. Mary saw and felt it all, her own health suffered from want of room, and from the anxiety caused by the difficulties of their position. A more favourable locality was earnestly sought for, and a Catholic lady of the neighbourhood offered to sell to them the Park Hotel. The amount asked frightened them, but Dr. Wiseman strongly advised them to purchase it, and promised to pay the interest for three or four years, in the hope that some generous and charitable souls would come meantime to their assistance.

Father Saulet went with M. d'Osseville to offer a lower sum, and when that was refused he was on the point of rising and breaking off the bargain, when the Count, anxious to see his daughter in a more favourable locality, exclaimed, 'I will myself pay the difference.' He also engaged to rent for their accommodation a piece of ground contiguous to the Park Hotel, which was only leasehold. The contract was signed on the first Friday in October, and during Benediction the religious sang a fervent *Te Deum* in thanksgiving.

The Count now prepared to return to France. His farewell to his daughter was truly pathetic; regarding her with deep affection, he said, 'Adieu, my child, I may hope to embrace you once more, but I shall never see you again.' His words came true, for when Mother St. Mary returned to France, he was totally blind.

All was now changed into active preparation for entering into possession of the hotel on the 11th of October, and as soon as the furniture was sold off, Mother St. Mary went to preside over the arrangements. Park Hotel is a large irregular mansion, part of which has some claim to antiquity; it has about seventeen acres of pleasure ground round it, and the lawn in front is closed in on the left by a wood. The country in the neighbourhood is undulating, and was at that time but thinly inhabited. The house had been a family hotel where parties of pleasure from London spent the day; previously to that it was a favourite resort of George III, who made use of it as a kind of ministerial rendezvous, and in a room which long served as the boarders' refectory, deliberations on public affairs were once held. It was curious to see a house connected with such associations converted into a Convent, and to find the old-fashioned ball room now become the chapel of the community.

The first Mass was celebrated on the 19th of October. The chapel was a large room divided into two compartments, and at first only one person came from outside to attend Mass in it. Within a couple of years the place became too small for the congregation.

Chapter XII

Opening of the School. The Cholera. General view of the work in 1850.

Father Saulet's return to France came to mar Mother St. Mary's happiness in her new orphanage. He left with them as his successor, the Rev. Father Vesque, whom he called 'his other self,' and from that moment this young missioner devoted his time and whole life to the work of the orphans. Yet, accustomed to the grave maturity and self possession of Father Saulet, it was not without some misgivings and much submission of judgement that Mother St. Mary saw herself at first placed under the care of one whose manner and appearance differed in many points. Extremely youthful in look, slight and diminutive in stature, timid and shy in manner, with nothing either winning or imposing to the eye, the contrast was great; but the selection which the Superior had made was fully justified by the result. Father Vesque gave proof both of virtue and talent in the fulfilment of his charge, until called away by the Sovereign Pontiff to rule over a very trying diocese in the West Indies, where he soon expended his remaining energies in the cause of religion.

The only step which the nuns could at first venture to take towards establishing an orphanage, was to open a day school; for as they themselves were only living on assistance supplied by La Delivrande, they could not afford to take in any orphans. The first who came to attend the day school were two little ragged children of the ages of seven and of two and a half years. Within a short time, however the little school numbered twelve pupils, as poor as the first comers, and even of their small pittance the Sisters had to give to those who were only a little poorer than themselves. One day two ancients of the school were observed holding a consultation in a corner, which ended in the younger giving her portion of bread to the most starved-looking of the other children, and then going to share her sister's morsel.

Days and weeks passed, and no orphan appeared; with how great satisfaction then must not the first have been at last welcomed, on the 4th day of November. Mother St. Mary assembled all the community to receive her, with her own hands presented her to our Lord in the chapel, at the feet of our Lady, would yield to no one the care of dressing the little stranger in the uniform which she had herself prepared. Each orphan who afterwards entered was received with equal tenderness by her maternal heart. Christmas speedily came round, and the little day-scholars were sharp enough to let their teachers know that at the Protestant schools on 'boxing day' the children had clothing and other things given to them. The poor nuns were quite unprepared for this appeal, but they applied to the inexhaustible charity of their friends in France, and soon large boxes containing old dresses, old bonnets, &c., arrived from Caen, La Delivrande, and Honfleur, to the great amusement of the custom-house officers when they were inspected. Skilful fingers soon gave new shapes and new attractions to old things, and on Christmas Eve the little scholars filed out in their fresh dresses to the words of their hymn:

Joyful, joyful,
Oh, that will be joyful.

Who could have imagined that so modest a demonstration as this could excite fear, anger, and jealousy in the breasts of the Protestants? The clergyman himself came to reproach the religious with having admitted children expelled from his own school. The Sisters maintained their right to receive the poor and helpless, and finding them both firm and fearless he withdrew discomfited. But the next day he stationed himself at their gate, threatening and taking down the names of the children who came. He then went to their parents and gave them the alternative of either withdrawing their children or else losing the weekly allowance of which he had the distribution. The newspapers also took up the matter, and the *Churchman* and *Church and State Review* inveighed against the poor nuns who had dared to come to teach and help the poor. One letter which was published related how the parson had accused them of injustice to himself, for whereas he was obliged to exact one penny per week for each child, they actually fed the children who came, and it was said gave a shilling weekly to each one, a crime which they might have been perfectly willing, but which they were wholly unable, to commit. The only evil effect of this passing storm was that the parents grew frightened, and in most instances removed their children, five alone being left. It would have been desirable to withdraw these little ones from such petty malevolence by receiving them into the house, but promises of help had not as yet been realized, and Mother St. Mary, though still confident in the ultimate success of the work, had to wait in much-tried but unfailing patience for the appointed time in which she was to exercise her active charity. Meanwhile she was, under the guidance of her new director, making rapid progress in virtue. Her health, which had greatly given way during the last three years of her stay at La Delivrende, was still very feeble. But yet taking advantage of every improvement, and even anticipating it, Father Vesque obliged her to rise at the sound of he first bell, preside at all the exercises of the community and deprive herself of several little comforts which her delicate constitution seemed positively to demand. Her obedience was admirable, the slightest directions of her spiritual guide were implicitly followed, and so much did God bless this submission, that mortifications, which would naturally have been injurious to her health, seemed on the contrary to strengthen it. Indeed the Assistant, who had been charged by the Mother General to watch over their Superior's health, taking alarm at what she was required to do, and fearing some rashness in so young a director, thought it right to caution him against permanently weakening the Reverend Mother's constitution. In sending her letter to Father Vesque, Mother St. Mary added these words: 'I let you have this note, Father, though it pains me to do so; be not influenced by that which affection alone dictates, for your penances do me good rather than harm.' The chaplain with his usual humility, thanking the Assistant for her charitable advice, begged her to examine for herself whether Mother St. Mary's health had really suffered from what he prescribed. If it had not, he begged permission for her to continue what God had evidently blessed; and as the Assistant confessed that Mother St. Mary was unusually strong, the latter was allowed to continue her mortifications with fresh ardour, saying: 'When Father Vesque concedes any point to me I am ill; when he refuses it I am well.' In illustration of her perfect spirit of obedience we give the following instance, though it belongs to a different date. During a visit of Father Saulet, Dr. Wiseman was invited to dinner. On sitting down to table he expressed a wish that Mother St. Mary should join them in the repast. She represented to him that her rule forbade eating with strangers, but when he gave her a formal and positive injunction, she immediately obeyed. As Father Saulet sat at the other end of the table, he did not observe what had taken place, and by most significant looks intimated his surprise and disapprobation. After Dr. Wisema's departure, he expressed his displeasure in very strong terms, but she, though deeply feeling his reproof, would not say a word in self- exculpation. One of the nuns afterwards reported the whole matter to Father Saulet, but the Mother Superior herself never alluded to the subject.

While she was thus a constant example of obedience she also sought to train up her daughters in its practice. She had the rare talent of inspiring the love of sacrifice, and could bind up with one hand the wound which duty had led her to inflict with the other. All that they did or suffered, their labours, privations, enjoyments were shared in common, and in after years Mother St. Mary used to recall to her daughters the fervour that had distinguished the early days of foundation. All loved her so tenderly that their inmost hearts were, so to speak, open to her inspection, and peace and happiness reigned in the religious family.

In February, 1849, the President of the Society of St. Vincent of Paul sent them several orphans, and their joy would have been unclouded but for the remembrance how near the time for the elections was at hand.

Father Saulet came, and in the name of the mother-house claimed the Foundress again according to previous promise and arrangement; the good Mother whilst preparing for her departure observed that her successor would make amends for her incapacity. But God had ordained otherwise. Fearing that the enterprise so lately undertaken would break down if its head were thus early withdrawn from it, Father Vesque, the Mother Assistant, and Mother St. Mary ad Nives, united in so strong an appeal to the Superior against her removal that they brought over Father Saulet to their own view. They added that Mother St. Mary was just beginning to be known and appreciated, and that a change now would produce an unfavourable impression on those who had begun to take an interest in the work. Father Saulet promised to place the matter before the community, and advise them to give up the idea of proposing her as Superior General. This decision was received with great joy, and a petition was drawn up and addressed to the chapter of the mother-house to that effect. The religious of La Delivrande gave an example of disinterestedness in acceding to the request, and sacrificing their hope of seeing their beloved Superior resume her place once again, so that Mother St. Mary was left to carry on the undertaking begun. She had always felt a strong desire to have the feasts of the Church celebrated with all possible solemnity. But in an heretical country more especially she was convinced of their usefulness in drawing converts towards the Church by speaking to the heart, as well as to the eye, and she longed to pay to her dear lord some little of that honour which so many denied Him. In this desire she was most earnestly seconded by the good chaplain whose taste was often called into requisition. On Palm Sunday she had the satisfaction of arranging a procession along the cloister in which some of the faithful took their part, for the parish of Norwood was now beginning to grow. Each Sunday she counted the number of those present at High Mass and saw the greater part of them fulfilling their Easter duties in the Convent chapel.

In acknowledgement of her great devotion to St. Joseph, Father Quiblier had sent her a large statue of her favourite Saint, while another of our lady Immaculate arrived in time for the month of May. It was enshrined in a little arbour ornamented with moss and flowers, and each day the religious and orphans repaired thither in procession singing the Litany with all the fervour of their hearts. At this period Dr. Wiseman published an appeal to the charity of the Catholics of England in favour of the orphans, and established a Society for the purpose of defraying the expenses of maintaining them.

Meanwhile the good Mother soon found another occasion for manifesting her zeal for the glory of God in the celebration of the feast of the most Holy Trinity, when the rule prescribed a procession during the singing of the Athanasian Creed, but which the annual secular retreat had always prevented their carrying out at La Delivrande. The words round Park Hotel now rang with the notes of the *Gloria Patri*, while the Reverend Mother, transported with joy, took part in the procession and chanting.

A very painful trial was close at hand by which God designed to perfect the work at Norwood and purify the souls of those engaged in it. At the renovation of vows on the 6th of August, 1849, the feast of the Transfiguration, Father Vesque had dwelt with especial fervour and solemnity on the necessity of bearing the cross, and it seemed as though his words were expressly directed to prepare his hearers for the cross which God was about to lay on them. In the evening of that very day the cholera, which had appeared in the neighbourhood, attacked the inmates of the Convent. The first sufferer was Mother St. Mary ad Nives, who as the only English member of the community was specially useful. Within a few hours she was in imminent danger and five others were seized. Earnestly did Mother St. Mary call on the Faithful Virgin, and a vow was made to take charge of another orphan if the sufferers were spared. While the Sisters still in health were attending on the sick, the Reverend Mother, according to a principle laid down by a good missionary, 'That the spirit of regularity is not violated if even but one follows the exercises,' went with a postulant to each observance, to the meditation, the examen, the refectory, saying the fixed prayers and responding to them, and in a word multiplying herself that each duty might be carried out in its proper order. At the same time she was careful to prevent any sadness from weighing down the hearts of her daughters, while her own confidence in God never flagged. Even when the medical attendant declared one evening that he did not expect to find Mother St. Mary ad Nives alive the next day, she still placed her trust in the Faithful Virgin, and not without reason. On the feast of the Assumption all the sick were completely cured, and the English Sister sufficiently recovered to come down to the community and hear Father Saulet's letter, in which he endeavoured to console them for her presumed death. One was able to accompany on an organ lately given them, the *Te Deum*, which all sang with feelings of the deepest gratitude.

Efforts were being made at this time to withdraw the Catholic children in the workhouses from Protestant hands, and to place them in institutions where their faith, their only inheritance on this earth, would be safe. Father Quiblier, ever anxious to forward the work he had so much at heart, had obtained a promise, unfortunately never to be realized, that ninety Catholic children in the Marylebone Workhouse should be passed on to Norwood, and Mother St. Mary prepared the house with the utmost care to receive them. Dormitories were set up in every practicable place, and the religious were dispersed into different parts of the house. She herself set the example by giving up her room to make a dormitory, and going among her dear orphans, of whom she constituted herself mistress. This obliged her to rise earlier, to be able to superintend their dressing and other duties. In winter, when the Sister who had that charge was ill, she more than once lighted the class fire, made the visit of order, heard the repetition of catechism, and showed in every point what a religious of the Faithful Virgin ought to be. Meanwhile the day school had more than recovered its former number of pupils, and one of the greatest pleasures of the good Mother was to teach these poor little ones their religion. The boarding-school at that time contained only eight pupils, who were also objects of her maternal care. Many of the young ladies brought up by her had entered the religious life, some in other orders, in England and elsewhere, and one of them is now at the head of a large Convent in England.

In February, 1850, eighteen orphans arrived, sent by Dr. Wiseman, after a collection in favour of the families of those who had died of the cholera. Several others applied for admission, but the resources of the Convent were inadequate for their maintenance, and they were, to the grief of the Reverend Mother, rejected. In the most touching terms she described to the community the misery of many poor children around them, and in order to encourage the observance of the strictest poverty and at the same time excite their faith, she promised in their name to receive one child who had been refused, if each nun would set to work to keep the little orphan in question. The terms were one farthing a day, saved by each religious, but if any article belonging to the house were broken, it must be replaced from the fund in their little treasure box. As many were the children of respectable parents in reduced circumstances, their misfortunes were more keenly felt, and of this class there has always been a large number in the house.

But though cheered onward by many consolations, Mother Ste Marie's path was still thorny, as the following letter from Father Vesque will amply show:

'Your retreat has passed as I expected; you must carry the cross to become more supernatural. Your nature must die (and we cannot die without suffcring), that it may rise again to the supernatural life which God requires of you. Do not fear. Your Spouse will not allow you to be tempted above your strength; but seek not eagerly to be delivered. Thank God that you have not had a harder struggle, and when you feel your weakness repair to the feet of the Faithful Virgin, ask her to tell you how much she has suffered, without complain or murmur– if you can.'

Chapter XIII

Agitation in England. Croydon Mission. Mother St. Mary in France. New Orphanage at La Delivrande. Death of Count d'Osseville.

The dormitories at Norwood were now well filled, and the class-room crowded with scholars, yet the latter could very easily be turned into a dormitory, and more space be thus obtained if only a new class-room were built, when therefore a valuable gift of £200 was sent by one of the Reverend Mother's relations, she at once asked permission from her superiors to devote it to this object. The opening of the new room was a great holiday for the children, who marched into it in procession, bearing the statues which had been put up in their former class-room. Dr. Wiseman often visited them in it, showing the warmest interest in the children, and when summoned to Rome at the time of the establishment of the Hierarchy, he came once more on the 6th of August to say good-bye to his favoured Convent. There was a cloud for the first time on the faces of the little ones as they welcomed him. They presented, as their parting gift, an alb which they had worked, and on which were embroidered the words, 'Father of the orphans, pray for us; pray for your orphans of Norwood.'* The kind Bishop immediately blessed the alb, and wore it at the ceremony of Confirmation which followed. He also preached what, as he remarked, was his first sermon in French to the religious, and received the renovation of their vows. Before he left, the kind Prelate blessed the children in general, and while he laid his hand on each little head, the voices of the children broke down in the chorus that they were singing. This, however, was not destined to be the last visit of Dr. Wiseman, for he returned soon amongst them as Cardinal, to show himself still the orphan's kind friend and father. When his life was threatened and some caution was necessary in going about, he managed to escape from the noise and bustle of London, and spend a few hours of calm among the religious at Norwood. During the agitation which followed the establishment of the Catholic Hierarchy, the Convent was not left unnoticed. On the 5th of November, a noisy procession, bearing effigies of the Pope and the Cardinal, approached the Convent gate, and halted for some minutes. The rabble were beginning to climb over the fences when the police interfered, and so the demonstration ended with a large bonfire, in which different effigies were burnt, and a great many fireworks were let off to the great delight of the children in the Convent.

While, in 1848, the need of fresh funds to build a separate infirmary was felt, they found their supplies diminished, for the benefactors who had

*In his last illness the Cardinal gave directions that he should be interred in the alb given him by the Norwood orphans.

undertaken the maintenance of some of the orphans were, for different reasons, unable to continue their donations. Thus the expenses of some seven children fell unexpectedly upon the Reverend Mother's hands, yet she had not the heart to turn them adrift. During the three years which had elapsed since the commencement of the orphanage one hundred and seven children had been received. Of this number, twenty-eight had been prepared for the sacraments, and eleven had been baptized. Mother St. Mary had another good work in her mind, the establishment, namely, of a 'Home', in which young girls, when out of situation, might be supported for a time, and preserved from moral contamination, and she longed for an opportunity of founding such an institution. Many conversions had taken place in their quiet little chapel at Norwood, and every Sunday two hundred persons were crowded into a room which could not comfortably have held one hundred. Regular instructions were given by the chaplain, and the music at High Mass and Benediction was sung by the religious and the children.

The earnest request made by a poor Irishman that the Sisters would admit his three boys into the orphanage and teach them, clearly indicated the urgent necessity of beginning a boys' school. Mother St. Mary undertook to furnish a teacher and the books, slates, fire, &c., requisite, and the chaplains agreed to provide a classroom from their already very limited accommodation in their small presbytery, which had been the stable of the former hotel. The Reverend Mother extended her charity also to the neighbouring town of Croydon. It was found that an aged priest lived there, who was almost bedridden, and who having formerly spoken English, French, Spanish, and Latin, now in his second childhood, blended all these into a sort of fifth and utterly unintelligible language. He had the charge of a very small chapel where a few Catholics attended, and where everything was in a very poor and neglected state. The zealous chaplain arranged to undertake the charge of this impoverished mission, trusting that in his kindness the Bishop of Bayeux would consent to send another priest. The chapel was in want literally of everything, even the sacred vessels were wretched; but Mother St. Mary generously shared with the new mission their very moderate riches at Norwood. The vestments were cleaned and put in repair, and the orphans went every Sunday to assist in singing at Mass. But the next want felt was that of a school, and this want cloistered nuns could not supply.[1] In this emergency, the best and most advanced of the orphans was selected, and sent three times a week to Croydon, to teach a class for two hours. But the distance was too great, the weather too often unfavourable, and the time insufficient to admit of this being more than a temporary arrangement, and on each occasion the Mother Superior watched with considerable anxiety the little teacher depart on her mission. After some time a respectable person agreed to reside at Croydon, to lodge the orphan in her small home, and to be a guide and protection to her.

[1] After Mother St. Mary's death, one great object of her desires was realized in the establishment of uncloistered Sisters.

Norwood, where several religious were obliged to sleep on mattresses laid upon the floor, for want of room in the dormitories. This little account was rendered in common, and each Sister, with simplicity and humility, suggested the ways in which she thought she could save; and while the good Mother listened and encouraged, poverty and generosity were at once fostered, and the zeal of all was inflamed when they saw how much they could do for the interests of Jesus.

At this time Cardinal Wiseman wrote to propose to Mother St. Mary a foundation in another part of England, earnestly pressing her to take charge of an orphanage under the patronage of a Catholic committee who undertook to maintain eighty orphans. She would most gladly have accepted the offer, but the excessive prudence of Father Saulet in not encouraging a further development of the Institute, led to the refusal of his consent. Father Vesque earnestly desired this extension, but distrustful of his own experience or judgment, he bowed to the age and maturity of Father Saulet. At the same time he urged the Reverend Mother to rely with a firm faith on the goodness of God, Who, even if He designed to grant them this foundation, would require greater suffering in preparation for it. In proof of his interest and esteem, Cardinal Wiseman paid a visit to the community at La Delivrande, and knelt before the miraculous statue of which he had heard so much at Norwood. During his visit the Cardinal again recurred to the question of the proposed foundation, strongly urging its acceptance, and Mother St. Mary made another effort with the Father Superior, but once more without success, and she was obliged, with considerable regret, to refuse it. Father Vesque again consoled her by representing that the will of God was in the matter, and that at all events their humility and obedience were secure, while God, as the Father of the orphans, did not stand in need of the services of either of them.

As the number of orphans at La Delivrande was now increasing, it was necessary to erect a separate building for them. The views of the Reverend Mother were again thwarted by those who should have most supported her, so that what would naturally have been an occasion of rejoicing to her, was made a fresh source of pain and vexation. Yet those only who enjoyed her fullest intimacy could perceive the suffering that was repressed beneath the usual smile of her countenance, or the gay rejoinder with which she gave life to the recreation of the community. She was naturally very cheerful, and this, as Father Faber remarks, is a great help to sanctity, besides often supplying the place of physical strength.

Her interest in Norwood caused her to feel some anxiety and regret when she learnt that the arrangement of the new dioceses would withdraw her Convent from the immediate patronage and direction of Cardinal Wiseman. She had not yet made acquaintance with Dr. Grant, and did not know that she would find in him a second and not less kind protector. A letter from the new

In this way for many months twenty-five children were regularly taught by one or two orphans, sent in turn every week from the orphanage.

Early in 1851, Father Saulet wrote to announce the decision of the chapter of the mother-house that the usual election should be advanced from February in 1852 to the June of 1851. The Superior, therefore, arrived in April, and having assembled the Sisters, explained that Countess d'Osseville's health threatened a stroke of apoplexy, and that it was deemed advisable Mother St. Mary should return to France. She at once complied, though in addition to her anxiety about her mother, she felt much pain in leaving a work which had just begun to bring forth such abundant fruit. The spirit and motive of her religious life shine forth in her few parting words: 'The first thing I ask of you is the spirit of self-sacrifice which is the basis of our work; sacrificing ourselves for our children and for the general well-being of the house. Self-sacrifice every hour, which leads us always to consider rather the general good than our personal convenience. Secondly, I recommend care and attention in preparing and superintending the exhibition of the children's work. You know it is the first, and the Cardinal has strongly impressed on us the importance of its producing a satisfactory impression. I need scarcely enjoin on you obedience to the two Mothers who remain. I trust to you for accomplishing punctually all they recommend. Be united, bear and forbear. If you detect some faults in a Sister, attribute it rather to want of strength than to want of will, and show kindness to her. Help to correct her defects by the gentleness of your manner, instead of allowing yourselves to be provoked by them. We all cause each other abundant annoyance, so we must all bear with one another. Receive the Sisters who will be sent to you with all charity, remembering what you yourselves felt on leaving your country; be doubly, therefore, kind and indulgent towards them.' She then returns once more to enforce the lesson of self-sacrifice, of living and working for the orphans.

Immediately on her arrival at La Delivrande, Mother St. Mary wrote to her spiritual children to announce her safety and wonderful state of health. On Sunday she was elected Superior General, and Mother St. Aloysius Gonzaga was named Superior of Norwood. Then overcoming her repugnance to this fresh call of duty, the good Foundress took advantage of the temporary amelioration of her health to resume regular observance, and to labour for the benefit of the orphans at La Delivrande. Her plan of education had become more exact and methodical, she had acquired greater experience, was never ashamed to learn, and turned to account all that she observed. Every duty was carried on with great vigour under her care, and complete uniformity established in the two houses. She carefully cherished mutual sympathy and interest between La Delivrande and Norwood, by the help of their recreations among other means; and every month the Sisters at the former Convent gave her a note of the points on which they had been able to economize in behalf of

Bishop, written with the delicate tact and thoughtful attention which were parts of his character, at once inspired her with a confidence which subsequent events deepened into filial affection and religious veneration. She heard with joy how paternal an interest he had already taken in the orphans, and how soon he had won their hearts.

In the spring of 1852, the good Mother had the satisfaction of placing the children in their new orphanage, where increased space admitted of better regulations being made. Mother St. Mary, however, was determined to guard against the danger of their improved comforts and accommodation unfitting the orphans for their future position in life. She had a particular talent for making them contented with, and even glad of, their humble rank, and though they shed bitter tears on leaving the house, they felt that a mother's heart was still following their career, and ready to welcome them again whenever they could spare time to come and see her. In July of this year the Sovereign Pontiff granted a plenary indulgence on the usual conditions for each visit to the little Norwood chapel, and another of seven years to those who contributed to the orphanage. Nor was this all. When Mgr. Talbot told him that a subscription had been opened to help the orphanage in England, Pius IX, sent an offering, and wrote an autograph letter to Mother St. Mary, containing his most warmly -expressed approbation, and his paternal blessing on her work. A supernatural grace attended the death of the first religious buried in the little cemetery at Norwood. An orphan was lying at the point of death, unable, through loss of speech, to make her confession. Mother Ste. Matilde, after bringing a blessed taper to place beside her during her agony, felt interiorly moved to offer her life instead of the child's, and thus enable her to receive the sacraments. Her holocaust was accepted; for the orphan recovered her speech and made her first Communion, but within a few days after Mother Ste. Matilde expired, and the taper which she had prepared for the orphan was burnt beside her own death-bed. Her habitual devotedness had inspired the children with such a feeling of veneration for her, that they all endeavoured to get possession of something which she had worn.

During the month of July Mother St. Mary made a short visit to Norwood, and returned to La Delivrande in August to find a new sorrow awaiting her. Her venerable father had been, as we have remarked, afflicted with blindness, which he bore with the utmost resignation. On the 29th of October, after attending Mass and receiving Holy Communion, he returned to his house, close to the chapel, and, when getting into a bath, was struck down by the bursting of an aneurism. He exclaimed, 'I am dying, but God's will be done.' A priest was hastily summoned, but the Count was insensible when the absolution was pronounced, and in a few seconds breathed his last.

The chaplain of the Convent went to announce the sad news to his daughter, who was walking in the garden. On hearing that M. Le Bedel asked for her, and that her father was ill, she immediately exclaimed, ‘Alas! He is dead—I shall never see him again.’ The painful task of the good missioner was facilitated by the resignation of the Reverend Mother, but she felt her father’s loss deeply. She had always placed complete confidence in his judgment on business matters, besides having a deep and well-merited veneration for his many virtues. She attended to every arrangement necessary for the funeral, as her father, being a founder, was buried in the Convent cemetery. She officiated at the Office for the Dead, and when the voices of the others failed she continued the chanting alone, with a tone of voice that drew tears from many eyes. She afterwards attributed to the prayers of her father several marked favours which she obtained.

Count Theodose d'Osseville

Mademoiselle Anne Renée de Valori (Contess d'Osseville)

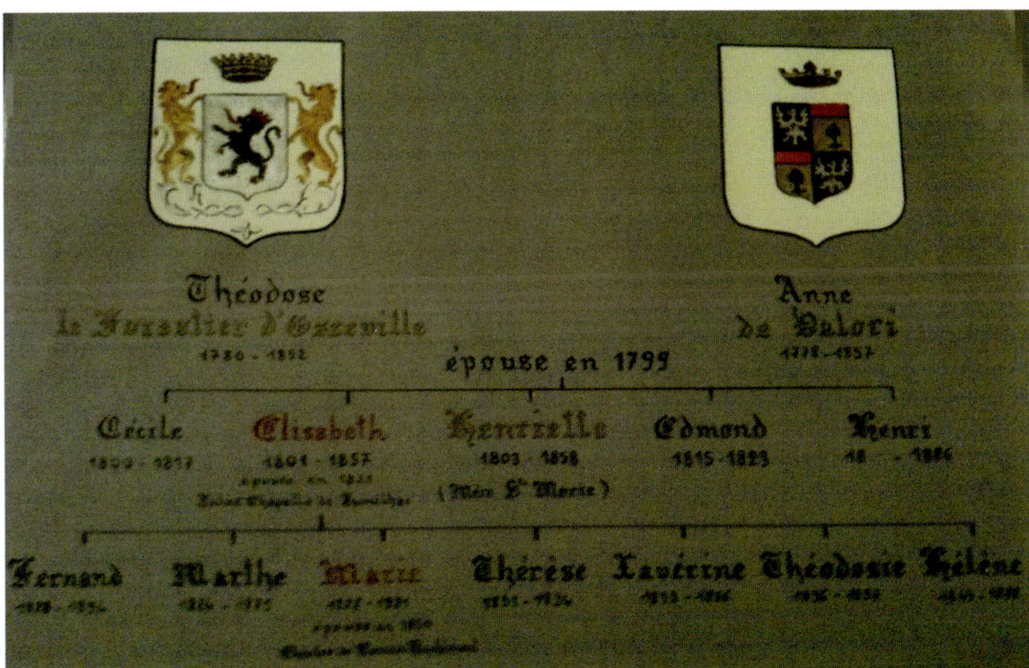

Family tree

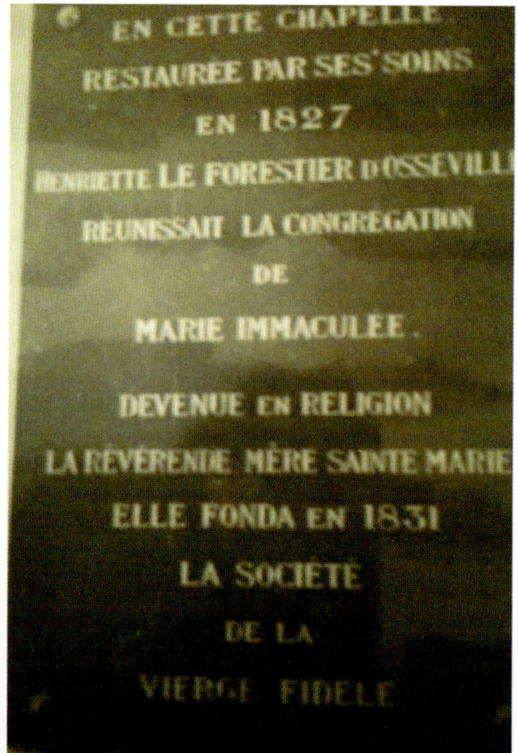

The church of Gavrus, where Henriette made her first Communion on Easter Tuesday of the year 1814.

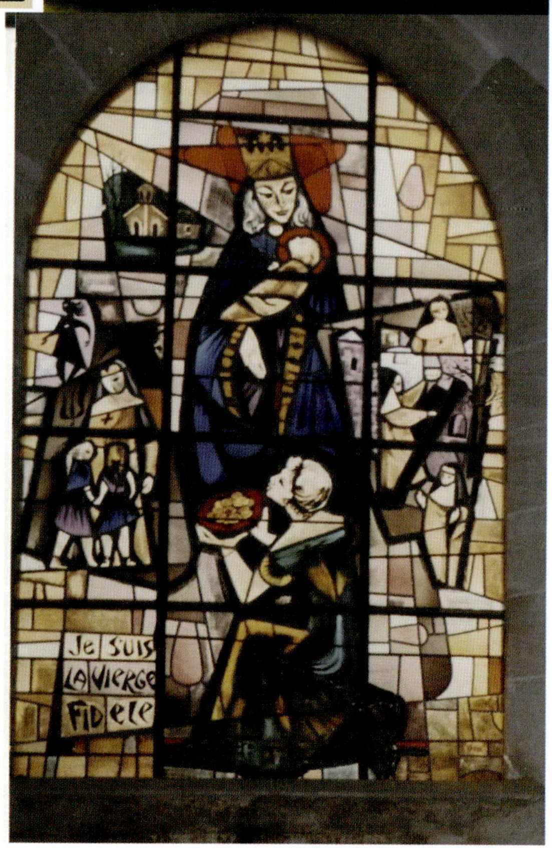

La Cathédrale de Bayeux

3 Septembre 1829 Départ pour Bayeux, où Henriette fait son noviciat, à La Charité. Elle reçoit le voile de postulante le jour de son arrivée. Melle d'Hendecourt est admise au postulat le 15 Septembre.

Les religieuses de la Charité sont installées, depuis 1826, dans une maison de la rue du Petit-Rouen.

Extrait de la "Notice de la Communauté de N.D. de la Charité de Bayeux :
" En 1829, la Communauté de N.D. de la Charité a l'honneur de former à la vie religieuse Melle Henriette Le Forestier d'Osseville, fondatrice du Couvent de la Vierge Fidèle, à La Délivrande."

The kitchen of the first house

The first house

Today

The miraculous cure of her sister in front of the Blessed Virgin of La Delivrande

Solemn procession during the time of the cholera. Every year this procession takes place on the 15th August, Feast of the Assumption.

Communauté de la Vierge Fidèle, La Délivrande, vers 1850

Norwood at the begining of 19th century

Norwood today

Chapter XIV

Resignation of Father Saulet. Visit of the Bishop of Bayeux. Death of Countess d'Osseville. Mary O'Leary.

Mother St. Mary became more and more anxious about the health of her daughters at Norwood, which she feared might suffer from the confinement and fatigue occasioned by want of room. In May, 1853, she declared that she would not cease to importune the Blessed Virgin until she had obtained from her a more suitable house for her children in England. She collected the names of all the Sanctuaries in which Mary has most displayed her power, and then, full of confidence in that faithful Mother, she wrote the following letter, to be placed on the altar of each shrine:

'My dear Mother, —Remember, you are the Faithful Virgin, the first Superior of this Institute, and that you have never been invoked in vain. As your Assistant —for with you I ought only to bear that title — I lay before you the wants of your two houses, which form really but one. Look, Mother, at your house at Norwood, at that little chapel which can not contain the Catholics who come every Sunday to attend Mass; and next at so many Protestants, who are first drawn by curiosity and then won by grace to the true Church. Look at the grief of our hearts to see Catholic orphans delivered up before our eyes to Protestant establishments, where they lose their faith and morals; look at the number of Protestant orphans who would receive the seeds of Catholicism in our houses, and yet hear us obliged to answer, "We have no room". Good Mother, your heart is more tender than ours, and ours cannot bear that suffering. Immaculate and Faithful Mother, remove the obstacles in our way; speak to your Divine Son, and grant us that a Church and orphanage should be built at Norwood. Oh, if it depended on me it would soon be done, though I am so unworthy. It depends on you, and you are goodness itself. Good Mother, I am full of confidence and love.

'You poor Assistant and spoiled child, who begs your blessing for all your daughters, and your orphans in France and England.

'(Signed) Mother St. Mary, Superior of the two Communities, and Assistant of the Blessed Virgin'.

Mary wished to try her daughter's faith still longer, and did not at once grant the prayer; but the good Mother's confidence continued unshaken. She persevered in her prayer, and at the same time employed all human means.

In the month of May, 1853, the Reverend Mother revisited Norwood with Father Saulet to conclude a matter of some importance. We have seen that Park Hotel had become quite insufficient to accommodate the number of orphans for whom application was made. The erection of another building presented great difficulties from the nature and disposition of the ground, as well as from other circumstances. So it was at first decided that they should leave Norwood, and seek out some more favourable spot. After visiting several places they found one property which seemed to possess the qualities desired. Father Saulet was particularly pleased with it, and advised that they should at once come to terms; he even wished a postscript to be added to the letter written to their man of business, urging him not to lose hold of so fine a property, but, if necessary, to send in by telegraph an offer to purchase. The Bishop of Bayeux having authorized the community at La Delivrande to advance the amount necessary for the purchase, all seemed quite settled, when, by the mysterious permission of Providence, the Father Superior suddenly changed his mind. He summoned the Mother Superior next morning, and required her to break off the bargain. This utterly unexpected change threw poor Mother St. Mary into a state of great perplexity. She felt strongly, and humbly submitted to him, the impossibility of now drawing back from the offer which they had made, showing that, according to English law, they exposed themselves to a prosecution for departing from a formal contract. She begged him at least to wait till Monday morning, that they might find out whether the agreement had been concluded on the Saturday or not; and meanwhile, faithful to the spirit of obedience, she sent directions to the agent to withdraw the bidding offered if the contract had not been completed, and if they could honourably retire from it. The answer received was that, owing to some flaw in the title-deeds, the agreement had not been concluded. But before its arrival Father Saulet bitterly reproached Mother St. Mary for her want of obedience, hastily left Norwood, and, on arriving in France, tendered to the Bishop of Bayeux his resignation as Superior of the Congregation. He wrote to acquaint the Reverend Mother with what he had done, and bade her apply to one of the Vicars-General for future direction in the affairs of her community.

It is difficult in this matter to account for the behaviour of Father Saulet. Very probably his mind had remained in an anxious and excited state ever since he found himself in conflict both with the Reverend Foundress and with Cardinal Wiseman in the question of beginning a new establishment; at all events, he felt himself being pushed forward against his will and against his own judgment, and perhaps fluctuated between his desire to see the English orphanage comfortably situated and his dread of the weight and responsibility of beginning what was virtually a new house, foreseeing in it the precursor of fresh undertakings. Though we cannot but see at once that Father Saulet was an exceedingly virtuous priest, with considerable aptitude for guiding souls, it appears equally evident that he was not a strongminded man; he had many prejudices and inflexible convictions of his own, and was inclined to take a narrow view of the spread of the Congregation in England. In these respects he was behind the age. Still in his abandonment of the post which he had so conscientiously filled, we trace the hand of the Divine Providence, which wished to unfetter the action of the struggling Institution that it might be shaped morc in accordance with the educational requirements of the day.

Not only did Mother St. Mary in her great distress of mind use every possible means to dissuade Father Saulet from taking this step, but Dr. Grant himself went to La Delivrande, and proving to him the Reverend Mother's entire innocence, made unavailing efforts to change a resolution so suddenly taken. Though he did all in his power to avert the evil consequences of the blow, he could not prevent a most unfavourable impression being produced in France. Rumour is always busy, and has a wonderful power in distorting and magnifying facts. One calumny asserted that to save appearances, Mother St. Mary had resold a property which had never been bought, and this report found its way even to her own family. Such, of course, was not the only ill-natured remark.

Though she felt this trial more deeply than any previous one, the good Mother would neither allow any of her daughters to offer an explanation in her defence, nor would she allow Father Saulet to be spoken of except with love and respect. Her reply to them was: 'We must love our Father; he has done us so much good. I may say that he has taken the life out of my heart, but I will love him as long as I live. God often makes use of those dearest to us to crucify us; and there are some secrets in Divine Providence that we must adore without understanding'.

That the Blessed Virgin was still watching over her children, the following remarkable favour will show. A little stream at Norwood, called the Effra, which, passes close by one of the class-rooms into a covered aqueduct, had suddenly swollen to such a height as to flood that part of the house, and block up its own course. The servant of the Convent suddenly slipped into the current as soon as it had been released again, and was on the point of being carried into the aperture, when Mother St. Mary fell on her knees, and cried out, 'O Faithful Virgin, save him'. At that instant a Sister, who stood on the sloping and slippery bank, placing her hand against a wall to steady herself, was able to lift the man on his feet again in safety.

A few weeks after this, the Bishop of Bayeux came to visit Norwood in fulfilment of a promise made to Dr. Grant. As was surmised, he wished to ascertain the truth or falsehooh of the various calumnies afloat in France. As soon as he returned home, he gave his ready consent to the enlargement of the Convent at Norwood. Before leaving Norwood, Mgr. Robin had said to Mother St. Mary: 'You may remain, but I should prefer you to return as soon as you can'. Her spirit of obedience led her to regard these words as an order, and she started the very next morning on her return to La Delivrande, where she arrived in September, 1853. Her presence was much needed, as some members of the community, having heard in the parlour of the reports that were current, in their ignorance of what had really passed, made certain inconsiderate reflections which deeply wounded the heart of their Superior; there was not one, however, who did not remain faithful to her.

Considerable anxiety was felt for a moment by the good Mother when she heard that Father Saulet had put before Father Vesque the alternative of remaining at Norwood and giving up his title of missioner of La Delivrande, or of renouncing his position as chaplain of Norwood to resume his functions as missioner.

The religious of Norwood will always owe a debt of gratitude to Father Vesque. His abnegation and devotedness to the cause of the orphan, his disinterested attachment to the house, and his valuable services as director and guide, cannot be detailed here. The privations he imposed on himself when the house was very poor and ill furnished are almost beyond belief, sharing in all the troubles, and entering into all the difficulties, in which he was ingenious enough to find always some remedy. At this juncture he wrote to Mother St. Mary in January, 1854: 'When we have not to direct events, we must look upon them as the accomplishment of God's will. It was evident that the last link which united the house of the orphans of La Delivrande to that of the mission could not long resist the storm. Let us pray that all may be for God's greater glory.' Father Vesque submitted his choice to the decision of the Bishops of Bayeux and Southwark. Dr. Grant loved him as a brother, and would have done everything possible to keep him in his diocese, and with the Bishop of Bayeux's kind interest in Norwood, it was speedily decided that he was to remain at Norwood, to the great joy of the good Foundress and her children.

Another cross befell Mother St. Mary in the death of her mother, the Countess d'Osseville. She had been already warned by two strokes of apoplexy, and on March 21, 1854, she was again seized, and died suddenly, yet not without being fully prepared. After her husband's death she made a handsome offering to La Delivrande. Her daughter, when returning from Norwood to La Delivrande, desirous of affording her spiritual children an example of fidelity to the rule, had declined to use the Bishop's permission to visit Gavrus in order that she might see her mother. A refusal which the latter was too saintly herself not to understand and fully approve.

A few hours before the aged Countess expired, the first of the Norwood orphans whom the community lost died, and Mother St. Mary consoled herself with the thought that she had gone to meet her benefactress on the threshold of eternity. The story of this young orphan, by name Mary O'Leary, is too interesting an episode to be omitted.

In the year 1848, when the misery in Ireland was so great that for many

Catholics the only escape from starvation was either flight from home or the denial of their faith, Patrick O'Leary made up two bundles of old clothes, told his children to take their shoes in their hands, that they might keep good to go to Mass in on Sunday, and then the father and mother, laden with their goods, set forward for the next port. The family consisted of three children, a boy of twelve and two girls, the youngest of whom Mary, the subject of our memoir, was ten years old. The man and his wife found work by going from farm to farm, but could never meet with steady employment. The nights were spent in outbuildings, or often by the roadside. During the outbreak of the cholera in 1849, Patrick O'Leary fell a victim to the first attack, but the poor mother never lost courage. Her eldest girl was fifteen, and with many prayers to God to bless her child, she left her in the first place she met with on the road where employment offered, and she continued to work in the field for her own support and that of her little boy and girl. The task, however, was too great for the strength, and one morning she said to her children, 'I shall not be able to get up today. You must go for a priest.' When the priest arrived at the poor barn which sheltered them, she had hardly a spark of life left in her. This, however, was not the worst, for the priest could only speak English, and she knew nothing but Irish. Then Mary wiped away her tears, and constituted herself interpreter between the dying woman and God's minister, and thus she prepared her to receive the last sacraments. The priest could not restrain his tears at beholding the zeal and faith of this little sister of charity.

The next morning the child knocked at the door of the presbytery to tell him that she was an orphan. 'Poor child', he answered, 'what will become of you?' 'I shall stay beside my mother until she is buried', she replied. 'And then?' 'Then I have to go to London, to give everything that belonged to mother to my sister, as she bade me do'. 'And then?' 'I don't know'. Alone in the streets of London! The priest could not bear to entertain the thought, and he told her to come back to him when she had fulfilled her mother's commission. He wrote to Norwood, offering to pay for the child and to become her adoptive father. At that time there were only a few orphans in the house, and so Mary was warmly welcomed when the priest brought her, and her rags were soon exchanged for the uniform in which Mother St. Mary was glad to see her clothed. Her good conduct soon placed her among those who were selected to inaugurate the Congregation of the Children of Mary. During this time her benefactor had to quit England, and he left her under the care of a charitable lady, who promised to replace him. Mary then saw herself on the point of being sent to a rich heiress, more as a companion than as a servant; but she was not elated with the prospect, and when these fine promises came to nothing, she evinced no disappointment. But now a real misfortune befell her, for her benefactress could no longer pay for her support at Norwood, and she was obliged to leave the loved asylum, not indeed to enjoy the good things of the world, but to taste its hardships. She was placed in service, and left full of gratitude for the little outfit she received. It had been arranged that she should have the free exercise of her religion. She was to attend Mass on Sunday, abstain on Friday, and go to confession once a month. A promise was even made that she should sometimes go and see the good Mothers at Norwood; and when this promise was at length realized, she accounted the distance of five miles as no impediment to her. She loved to render an account of her little money matters to the nuns, and she would ask them to purchase her clothes for her, saying that they knew better than she did what was fit and needful for her.

Later on, Mary O'Leary was placed as a nursery governess in France, and loved her two little charges as tenderly as she had loved her Mothers. One of them owed its life to her indefatigable care. For six weeks this poor little creature, struggling between life and death, would lie nowhere night or day but in Mary's arms. Her charitable imprudence led to the natural results. Her health was visibly affected, and from the moment they perceived this, her employers spared no pains to arrest the fatal consequences. But she, through fear of being a burden to them, had hidden as much as possible the rapid progress of her illness. Within a few months all hope seemed over, and it was thought that her only chance was to breathe once more the air of her beloved Norwood. So she returned to the arms of the mothers who had first received her, and became soon convinced that she had come to die there. But the prospect of death had nothing in it to alarm her. Rather did she love to speak of it, and of the joys of Heaven, and she never uttered a complaint during her illness. All was good, all was well, and the kind Mothers did too much for her. 'Do not tire yourself so; I am well as I am,' were the words addressed, a few minutes before she died, to the nun who was trying to raise her a little that she might breathe more freely. She caused herself to be supported that she might receive her Lord with more respect, and her last Communion was even more fervent than her first. In her lifetime she had wished to give everything she possessed to the House of the poor orphans, but this had been refused. She profited by her approaching death to repeat the request, asking them again to accept what she could leave as a token of her gratitude. 'Give all that I have to our good Mother;' and then she laid her head on the bosom of the nun who nursed her, pronouncing the holy names of Jesus and Mary with her last breath. Such was the orphan girl who welcomed, as Mother St. Mary loved to think, the Countess d'Osseville into Heaven.

Chapter XV

Mother St. Mary visits Norwood. The Abbé Rivière named Superior. The Hospital at Scutari.

Other deaths in Mother St. Mary's family soon followed upon that of the Countess d'Osseville. The Countess de Jumilhac lost one of her grandchildren and within a short time her second daughter, Therese, after a brief illness of a few days. With reference to her Mother St. Mary remarked, 'Amongst our many recent losses, not one has oppressed my heart so much as the death of poor Therese. Her image pursues me everywhere, and does not allow me a moment's rest. I really think she wants me to take her Purgatory upon myself.' In truth, a new burden of a very peculiar nature was being prepared for her. She must have felt very much surprise —if we take in the whole history of the past —on receiving a request from Father Saulet to admit into the novitiate a young person whom he destined for the foundation of a new community close to the mission chapel of La Delivrande. Although it was quite evident that this fresh establishment was intended to take up a rival position to her own, she at once, with the utmost self-denial, acceded to his proposal. When the new postulant showed a decided preference for the work of charity to orphans and entreated to be permitted to remain as a subject of Mother St. Mary, the latter would never consent to take any steps in the matter.

She assisted Father Saulet with her skill and experience whenever he consulted her as to the rules of the future community, and imposed silence on those of her daughters who, not sharing in the heroic perfection of her generosity and self-abnegation, felt an objection to the work expected of their Foundress. The variety of Mother St. Mary's mental sufferings had so greatly undermined her health that the approaching close of this triennium of her rule made her all the more long for repose, and she earnestly entreated her daughters to allow her three years respite, fully persuaded in her humility that another would repair the evils which she considered her incapacity and bad health had occasioned. But her community did not agree with her, nor could they resolve to release her from the charge of government, and on May 23, 1854, she was re-elected Superior General. She intimated her regret with the gentle words, 'What is it you have done? Had you but given me a little rest, my health would have been restored. But God's will be done.'

The Reverend Mother was shortly afterwards called to Norwood on important business. The Cardinal asked for a foundation in the Archdiocese of Westminster. New obstacles had arisen to their building at Norwood, and other properties had, in consequence, been proposed, one of these being Beaumont Lodge. Mother St. Mary placed the government of the house in the hands of the Assistants of the two communities and started for Norwood with Mother St. Aloysius Gonzaga, who had been appointed Local Superior of the latter house. While absent she thus enjoined those who replaced her : 'Recommend to our dear Sisters that they should listen to the spirit of faith and follow the line of duty, considering the glory of God in all things, the welfare of our children and the salvation of souls, more especially of those which are distinctly in trusted to them. My best blessing to the most self-devoted.' Alluding to Father Saulet she adds, 'Let us be strong and brave. Be assured, we have not had the last shock. Let us raise our hearts upward, looking to God. He will show us the path of duty, and will give us strength to follow it, even should we feel crushed to the very earth. You know all that my heart has suffered —all its affliction. Let us strengthen one another and not forget that others lean on us.'

Father Vesque persuaded her to take the opportunity of consulting an English physician. She had extreme repugnance to his treatment, and did not think it suited her constitution, but her obedience was blessed and her health restored beyond her expectation. She often repeated this fact as a proof that religious ought to leave the care of their health to their Superiors and seek no other physician than that of the house where they are, and should adopt in general the habits of the country in which they live. She combined great prudence with humility in treating the delicate question of a change of house, and it had been settled between the Bishop of Southwark and herself that, if within a certain time no property had been found, they were to consider it God's will that they should remain at Norwood. At the same time, the Cardinal pressed again for a new foundation, anxious that the orphans of St. Patrick should be placed under the care of religious, and that some others whose faith was endangered by the perversion of their guardian might be added to their number. Mother St. Mary wrote to the Sisters in France: 'You must pray a great deal; be ready to leave at the first sign of obedience. If the new plan fails, we shall have the merit of it all the same; but let us not put any obstacles in the way of God's designs.'

And later on, speaking of the property they had hoped to secure, she thus expressed her disappointment: 'Beaumont is sold. We begin to see God's will. Just as we were making preparations to move, they send us word that the property, which for three years had been advertised for sale, is bought. In this way, while we are begging God to show us if He wishes us to go there, He has answered the doubts which we felt on account of the many difficulties before us, and, as we followed the wish of Dr. Grant, we were sure of doing God's will, and therefore the news found us and left us —calm. We shall begin our search anew until the day fixed, and then, if nothing offers, we shall conclude that it is His will that we should remain here. It was the wish of our good Bishop of Bayeux, and in spite of the difficulties attending that plan, his desire has great weight with us. God will bless you, dear daughters, if regularity is flourishing among you. What good would it be to found houses where this was not the case? If you knew what I suffer when I see it violated. Let us be steeped afresh in that spirit.'

The religious had about this time worked and sent an alb to the Holy Father, and received from him this paternal acknowledgment:

'Your letter of February 9 as remitted to us with the beautiful alb sent in your name and that of your Sisters at La Delivrande. We express to you and to them our well merited gratitude; and to the sentiments of filial piety and devotion so warmly expressed in your letter, we reply by the assurance of our paternal favour towards you and your establishment. May the Saviour of the world, so full of tenderness, bless the labour and care with which you incessantly watch over the little orphans of the Catholic Church and save them from want. We praise, as it is our Apostolic duty to do, this your ardour in the salvation of souls. And may our Apostolical Benediction be to you the pledge of a heavenly reward, a benediction which in all tenderness and in the intimate affection of our paternal heart we give to you, beloved daughters in Jesus Christ, to your Sisters in France, and to all your little orphans.

'Given at Rome, May 6' 1854, of our Pontificate VIII.

'PIUS P.P. IX.'

At this time the community lost another of its members, who died during the singing of the *Te Deum* in preparation for the feast of the Assumption.

In August the Abbé Rivière, Vicar-General of Bayeux, the new Superior of the Convent of La Delivrande, paid a visit to Norwood and gave a retreat. During his stay the Mother Assistant at La Delivrande wrote to him, begging him to oblige Mother St. Mary, in virtue of obedience, to undertake the revision of her constitutions. Her diffidence was so great that such a command was necessary to urge her to this labour. She set to work, but could not continue, for she returned before the end of the month to La Delivrande, where the religious and the orphans gave her a very warm and joyous reception, the latter meeting her in procession at the chapel of La Delivrande, to testify the firmness of their attachment to her after all the unpleasant things that had been said. On the occasion of an act of flagrant ingratitude from one who had long received her benefits, Father Vesque writes to her : ' Let us try never to speak of the ingratitude of men. He for Whom we do all thing is not ungrateful. Those whom we call ungrateful, properly speaking, owe us nothing; it is not for them we work. Do not think I say this to dispense myself from the gratitude I owe you; it is a warning for your peace. Those who do good on earth are not happy if they wish for the gratitude of those whom they benefit.

Yes, this person has been most unjust; but we too have been unjust towards our good Master. Suffer, suffer, since He wills it so.'

Shortly after her return to France, Mother St. Mary received intimation from Norwood of Dr. Grant's appeal for five of the religious to be sent to the military hospitals at Scutari. She instantly despatched an express to solicit Mgr. Robin's permission, and this having been obtained, she assembled all her daughters and made a short but touching appeal to their zeal and devotedness, begging those who were ready for the sacrifice to give in their names on a slip of paper. Their answer to her appeal was unanimous. It may not be uninteresting to know the circumstances which compelled Dr. Grant to appeal on this occasion to a cloistered community whose end was not the care of the sick. During the Crimean war the Government had consented to send priests and even religious to the aid of the wounded. To have let the opportunity slip would have been to lose it for ever; to seize it was to remove many prejudices and, so to speak, to gain a victory. The number was fixed by the authorities at ten persons. The Bishop had only five whom he could send. Several applications being made in vain, he went to Norwood on Friday evening. ' I want Sisters,' he said to the Reverend Mother, 'and I have none.' 'My Lord,' she replied, 'you know we are in your hands.' 'They are,' he said, 'wanted at Constantinople to take care of the wounded.' 'That is not our work,' she answered, 'but if you find no other—.' 'I thank and bless you,' said the Bishop, much moved, 'and if I find myself still in want of any, you shall know in time before the day of departure, which is Monday next, October 23.' Sunday evening came, and yet no message; the religious concluded that the Bishop had obtained assistance elsewhere. But just as they were retiring to rest at nine o'clock, the rapid steps of a messenger were heard, who brought the following summons: 'I must have five of your sisters by seven o'clock tomorrow morning at London Bridge, ready to start for Constantinople.' It was not without emotion that the Mother prepared to obey. It seemed so strange an act to send her daughters to a far distant military hospital under a Protestant superior. Both she and Dr. Grant would have preferred waiting for Mother St. Mary's answer from France, but the hour of departure made that impossible. However, she well knew the Apostolic Spirit and the boundless charity, both of the Bishop of Bayeux and Mother St. Mary, and felt safe in anticipating their intentions. The whole community spent a few moments before the Blessed Sacrament, offering themselves up to God's will, and then the Mother Superior made her selection of four English and one French Sister, and before six o'clock on Monday morning the nuns, equipped for their journey, reached the Bishop's house at St. George's. The satisfaction, and even gratitude, of his Lordship were most marked. He was so kind, so full of forethought and paternal solicitude. Along with Father Vesque he accompanied them to the station, and waved a last blessing towards them as the train moved off.

As soon as Mother St. Mary heard of their departure she hastened to Norwood, bringing five sisters with her. On the steamer, between Havre and Southampton, she learnt that the stewardess had a son at Scutari, and promised to recommend him to her daughters, that the poor woman might have the consolation of knowing her son would not be entirely uncared for amongst strangers. We give the following extracts from a letter which she wrote to Mother St. Mary ad Nives who was at the head of the little band of nuns:

'My dear child, —My motherly heart longs to hear that you have received news of Norwood and La Delivrande. Poor dear children! Our thoughts are fully occupied with you. It gives me new life to hear of you. This morning your letter of the 10th reached us. Both Mr. Tetos and his wife are kindness itself, and will recommend you specially to the Sisters of St. Vincent of Paul, both at Paris and Constantinople. We find a universal feeling of interest about you that does our heart good. God is with you; do not doubt it, my dear child. Confide your difficulties and doubts to Him. Tell Him with childlike simplicity that you went to Constantinople for His glory, and that He must not allow you to tarnish it by any human motives. Your faith will prevent you from doing anything to mar the good impression that as Catholic and religious you ought to make. You are as a Mother to your religious Sisters. Oh! be a good mother to them, remembering how a child's heart dilates when she finds her mother kind and indulgent. Cover, therefore, with the cloak of charity all their slight blemishes... . Our little ones here are full of you. They want to follow you, that at least one for each religious may help to make French lint for you. The younger ones have undertaken by their little sacrifices to save the souls of "those great black-bearded soldiers." Do not overtax either your strength or your zeal; you may have long to work, and must not fail before your task is accomplished; but should God take any of you to your recompense, I could not quarrel with Him; on the contrary, I should envy her happiness and rejoice with Him and with her. ...You have heard all the French news direct from La Delivrande, and Mother St. Aloysius Gonzaga tells you what goes on in England; but you will not mind hearing twice how much Father Vesque thinks of and prays for his daughters in the East. He recommends you to be always modest and retiring, everywhere the last, following the example of the Faithful Virgin. Take your part in the meanest and hardest work, and let the worst share be yours, and God will bless you. Thank with all the effusion of my full heart the good Superior of the Sisters of St. Vincent of Paul for her kindness to you. She, too, is a mother, and will understand what we feel to see our birds so far from the nest, a nest, too that was caged. ...Dr. S —always sends us his papers: one of them gives an illustration of the fishwomen of Boulogne carrying off your luggage with enthusiasm from the steamer on your disembarking. God bless these good women.' Again, on December 2, she writes: 'I am told that a mail leaves for the East to-day. How can I resist sending a little greeting to each one? Yes, certainly; Mr. B— will be heartily welcomed at La Delivrande when he comes. By all means invite him, and I promise him a cordial reception. How could we fail to like him since he was so kind to you on your voyage? Thirty Sisters of Mercy start to-day to join you. They take with them a little box containing a small remembrance for each of you. Though of no great worldly value, a reliquary for each is a treasure indeed to those who have faith.'

Afterwards, hearing that none of her letters had reached their destination, she wrote on the 12th of December: ' I am so sad, dear child, to see by the letters addressed to your two Mothers on the 24th , that you have heard nothing form me, though I have written four or five times since you left. My heart is very full of you, and many a blessing and prayer I send after you. All your details interest us immensely. Little Marcelle was quite proud to think that you had nursed her wounded uncle, and Germaine seemed almost sorry her father was not wounded, in order that he might pass through your hands also. I am happy to see that you all get on so well with the Sisters of Mercy, and rejoice that the Reverend Mother from Bermondsey calls you "dear child." I do so like to feel you have a Mother, and as they say she is so prudent and so excellent, follow her advice in everything. You are right, the time you are now passing through will ripen you, and if with that you are very humble, you will at forty be a really good religious!... . For this end pray hard, listen to God's voice speaking within you—enter deeply into the inner life; in other words, place yourself in the hands of God under the guidance of His Divine grace in everything that you do. This habit can only be gradually acquired, but once attained it is very, very sweet.'

The stay of the Sisters at Scutari was only a brief one. They had passed six weeks in the hospital there nursing the sick and wounded with the tenderest charity, when the Sisters of Mercy in Ireland, having responded to the appeal of Dr. Grant, sent out their contingent of fifteen nuns, who arrived towards the end of December, to join the members of their Institution already working there. The mission of the daughters of the Faithful Virgin had therefore come to an end, and they returned to the practices of their own cloistered life. As the first Sisters had broken enclosure in the cause of charity to attend the cholera-stricken at La Delivrande, so these had gone forth to nurse the sick and wounded soldier. Their Superior had written to the Archbishop of Petra to announce their return, and his answer deserves insertion:

'Constantinople, 5th February.

'My dear Sister,—Your were already far from Scutari when you letter reached me. I was grieved for the sake of the poor sick men at your leaving the hospital, the maternal charity which accompanied your care was the greatest alleviation to their sufferings. It would seem that Divine Providence only wished to give you the means of comparing the exercise of charity towards the sick, with that which you have shown towards the orphans. Which then of the two is really richer and more fertile in merit? Devotedness in nursing the sick and wounded in the battle wears a brighter lustre in the eyes of the world, for it sees in it courage, self-sacrifice, and even heroism; and justly so, since the care bestowed by the hospital Sister is precious to Jesus Himself, Who has said that whatever is done for the poor, and still more for the sick, is done for Him. Yet if we examine more deeply into the matter, your office of Mother of the orphan has something in it yet more valuable and meritorious. To adopt a poor child deprived of all human protection and in danger of grovelling in ignorance and vice, and to form it to the practice of all virtue, is a good work which yields to none in merit or excellence. The hospital Sister relieves the bodily suffering of a fellow-creature, but she who is as a mother to the orphan trains up a creature to be worthy of God and of its duties in this life. You may then easily console yourselves that assistance in the hospital is no longer required of you.

'I pray God to pour His blessing on yourself, your children, and your labours.

'J. M. HILLEREAN.

'Archbp. of Petra, Vic. Ap. of Constantinople.'

Chapter XVI

Admission of St. Patrick's orphans. Father Vesque named Bishop of Roseau. His consecration and departure.

During the absence of her daughters in the East Mother St. Mary was busy negotiating with the committee in charge to obtain, at least for a time, the care of the orphans of St. Patrick's. We must not pass unnoticed the name of one who is entitled to esteem from all English Catholics. Mrs. Barnewall was the first who by her generous abnegation and active charity founded in England an asylum for about twenty destitute orphan children. For several years she supported them by her own efforts, and was at once their Mistress and their Mother. When she no longer felt equal to the task, she looked round for some religious community which would take charge of the good work begun by her. The Cardinal introduced her to Mother St. Mary, and after the admission of her orphans to Norwood, Mrs. Barnewall continued to encourage them by her favour and by frequent visits; and when the infirmities of old age prevented her using this influence, she bequeathed to Lady Georgiana Fullerton a work which bears the mark of especial blessing, for it has been observed that all the children rescued by her care and brought to Norwood either died a holy death, or have by their lives in the world proved themselves worthy of the solid Christian education they had received. Mother St. Mary wrote to a friend: 'We are going to ask to have charge of the children of St. Patrick's, even if they only remain with us for a time, as there is danger of their being exposed to harm, while the committee is making the necessary arrangements. I think our Lord will not be angry with us for doing this'.

The business which brought the Mother Superior to Norwood having been concluded, she returned to France, where in the month of May following she had the happiness to learn that the building of the orphanage in England was at last begun. In that month, Father Vesque wrote to her: 'All is now concluded. Dr. Grant has given his decision what we ought to build at Norwood. His Lordship says: "On this day I feel I ought no longer to defer my answer to the question put before me by the two Convents, and now I come to beg the Superior to be so good as to obtain the consent of the two communities that this Convent shall be built where you now are. May our dear Mother bless this answer which I have sent you, and may she be ever with us." To this I replied immediately, that we should thank the Blessed Virgin from our hearts for having led his Lordship to form the decision which he had announced. We are going to set seriously to work on the plans, and we hope to be able to begin this year'.

The climate of La Delivrande seems always to have been trying to Mother St. Mary's health, and soon after her return a complication of disorders reduced her bodily strength without enervating her indomitable energy of mind. Although in the summer of 1855 complete repose was declared to be absolutely necessary for her, she did not forego her supervision of the house, and during the day her bed was placed near the window, where she watched with interest the movements of the Sisters and of the children. While thus suffering she lost one of her most valued daughters at Norwood, Mademoiselle de Tolleville, Mother St. Philomena. This nun was of an ardent and generous temperament, from the first moment of her arrival in England she devoted herself to the children of the poor-school. As long as she could walk she managed to be among them, and even when she could take only a few steps at a time she would ask any nun who happened to pass by to help her on one of her short distances, until by a succession of such stages, she managed to reach the school-room, where by words or signs she made herself understood in an inexplicable manner. She spoke English with great difficulty, and said in her naïve French idiom: 'I pardon Providence everything but the confusion of tongues; oh, if I had but the gift of languages!' yet it certainly seemed that after a fashion she had this. There were little Irish children at her school who hardly knew a word of English, and still could comprehend and obey her, and even little Protestants when once they had seen her would go to no other school, and have no other mistress than the 'good lady'. The children under her care were generally very indigent, and the poverty of the community had enough to do to provide for the orphans, but her zeal managed to turn the oldest and strangest things to good account. As a wonderful instance of her influence in training children, we may mention that two little girls had been only a few weeks under her care, and were then removed for several years from all Catholic intercourse, notwithstanding which they retained so vivid a recollection of her virtue, that they afterwards returned to 'the religion to which that good lady belonged, and which must have been the right one'. She had habitually asked God that He would grant her to suffer during the night, and give her strength to work during the day. This prayer He doubtless heard, for any one who had been witness of her terrible oppression from asthma during the night, must have marvelled to see her the next day in her class as usual. Being very stout, she feared that she might occasion much fatigue and trouble in a long illness and 'take up room better occupied by an orphan', so she begged of God that her last attack might be short, offering to bear as sharp sufferings as He chose. In this also her Divine Spouse granted her generous and disinterested petition, for she was not a fortnight ill, but suffered fearfully at the close of her life.

Mother St. Mary returned to Norwood, where her health generally improved, and once again the religious had the satisfaction of seeing their beloved Mother able to fulfil all the duties which her office laid upon her. She found nearly one hundred orphans crowded into the house, amongst whom many new faces greeted her, as the elder children had already been sent out to situations and their places were filled by younger and more timid new-comers. Her contrivances to give them pleasure and find means of rewarding them soon gained every heart. She seized the occasion of the visit of Cardinal Wiseman, and of several other ecclesiastics, to arrange a fair of a novel description. With the exception of one stall, in which the orphans' needlework was displayed, and another of illuminated cards, all the stalls were accessible to the orphans, and a new currency established for the occasion, namely tickets bearing the number of good marks gained within a given time. There were plenty of toys, and sweets given by a kind friend, and articles of unknown value and beauty bought wholesale from a penny stall in the 'Faubourg St. Antoine,' all which were marked, not so many pence, but so many tickets. The visitors were much amused with the scene, and watched the children going about from one stall to another, laying out their tickets. A child, by no means one of the best behaved, was under the special patronage of the Cardinal, whom she justly considered her benefactor. Her whole fortune consisted in seven tickets, which, compared to the one hundred and fifty that some had, did not give her much to trade with. If Catharine had not much head, she certainly had a warm heart, so she went to the stall of little French pictures, and choosing the best which her seven tickets could buy, she, after some hesitation, offered it to her benefactor as a testimony of gratitude. The Cardinal was much pleased with the amiable trait of character thus displayed.

The last days of 1855 were saddened by the death of the Bishop of Bayeux, whom Mother St. Mary had found a friend and protector, and whom the orphans of Norwood still remembered as a kind father. Faithful to the inspiration of gratitude, they made a collection at their New Year's Day dinner to be given to the poor for the repose of his soul.

The close of 1855 found Mother St. Mary again in the house at La Delivrande, when she resumed her duties of Superior General, and continued them indefatigably as long as her health permitted. This, however, again failed. She first lost the use of her voice, and then from gout and other ailments she became unable to read and write. During this state of painful inaction she was most anxious to lay down a charge which she seemed to herself totally incapable of filling, and earnestly entreated that the elections fixed for May, 1857, should be advanced. This could only be done with the permission of the ecclesiastical Superiors, and Mgr. Didiot was hardly as yet installed in his diocese. Father Vesque therefore recommended her to await patiently the time fixed by the rule, or perhaps, with the permission of the Father Superior, to delegate her authority to some one as a temporary expedient. On the 11th of August he wrote to her as follows: 'It would certainly be a great relief to you to be delivered from the office of Superior, and I do not doubt that his Lordship and the Father Superior would accept your resignation. Inasmuch as it would deliver you out of some of your troubles, I should thank God. But if I love you, I also love the community the firm establishment of which the good God has laid upon you; and when I think of advancing by six months the inevitable crisis, which, come when it may, will always cause a serious embarrassment, I feel inclined to despair a little, if despairing could cure evils, or even repair a single fault. Away, then, with the dark thought, which only makes blacker what is already not too bright. The less clearly we see for ourselves, the more we should trust in the grace of God, Who said. "My daughter, thy faith hath saved thee". Let us go forward, then, hoping in His mercy. This is my motto and my only hope. The most ardent wish of my heart is that God may cure you and to obtain your cure I shall offer the Holy Sacrifice for you tomorrow; and when the intentions which are just now obligatory upon me are finished, I promise to make a novena of Masses in honour of the Immaculate Conception of the Queen of Heaven'.

Meanwhile earnest prayers were offered and repeated novenas made for the restoration of Mother St. Mary's health; after these she recovered her voice and strength sufficiently to acquit herself of her many duties. The direction of Father Vesque had been to her a source of great light and consolation, but of this she was now about to be deprived. During a visit paid to his family he was invited to preside at the ceremony of clothing for some novices at La Delivrande. Just as Mother St. Mary was preparing to go into the church a note was placed in her hand containing the painful news. She let the letter fall, and said to the Sister who accompanied her, 'Alas! Father Vesque is appointed to a bishopric, and that, too, at the other end of the world.' She, however, controlled her emotion, and allowed no traces of sorrow to overshadow the joy of the young novices. Anxious for the consequences attendant on the removal of one who had been their principal stay, she hastened to her children at Norwood. She had again lost her voice, but recovered it after a novena to St. Philip Neri. Most fervent prayers were offered up by the community and by the orphans, that their beloved Father might not be taken from them at a moment when the extension of the work seemed to make his presence doubly necessary. Father Vesque had written a humble letter of remonstrance to Rome, setting forth his reasons for being allowed to decline the post to which he had been appointed –the bishopric, namely, of Roseau, in Dominica, one of the West Indian Islands, a British possession, situated between the two French islands of Martinique and Guadaloupe. While he was awaiting an answer, Mother St. Mary wrote as follows to Madame Vesque, mother of the Bishop elect:

'My good Mother, —All hope is not lost. The Cardinal Prefect of the Propaganda has found one of Father Vesque's reasons sufficient to make him delay expediting the Bulls, and institute further inquiries, which may give greater weight to the difficulty in question; and as this is not a personal one, it has more chance of success. Providence seems to have heard so many little voices raised up to ask that their Father and protector might remain. We must not flatter ourselves too much, but it is such a relief to have a little hope. I show our Lord unceasingly how necessary his presence is here, at least for a few years more. Our little ones are charming: they will not commit the smallest sin this week, that God may have pity on them. Our good chaplain arrived here yesterday, rejoicing in his father's happiness. His humility is admirable; he is as desirous to remain hidden and unknown as others often are to raise themselves above their fellow-men. To tell you the truth, it is this that makes me fear the most. Has not God said, "He who humbleth himself shall be exalted?" But we both think, perhaps He might wait a few years before He exalts him. The Cardinal has not answered the letter written in your name, in which I employed every argument my affection for you could suggest. Alas! We poor women can do nothing in these great affairs... . I enjoy the moment of hope my letter will give you all. What a happiness if in a little time I can write, "He will remain". Pray hard, and get others to pray, and be sure you will always find a devoted heart in

'Mother St. Mary.'

Singularly enough the final nomination of Dr. Vesque, whose name was Michael, arrived on the feast of the Archangel. It had formerly been a fête day for the orphans, but this year it was to be a day of sorrow. Bishop Grant, who loved Dr. Vesque like a brother, and deeply regretted losing him, went to announce the tidings to the children. On seeing him approach alone, and full of thought, they at once guessed his errand, and burst into tears and sobs. The good Bishop said gravely: 'Children! Formerly the friends and relations of the martyrs encouraged them in the combat: will you be less generous? No, my children, unite your sacrifice to theirs'. Eighteen months later Dr. Grant came again among them, sad and oppressed, and, pointing in silence to the picture of their much loved Father, he knelt down and said with them the *De Profundis*. But we anticipate.

A few days after his nomination, Mother St. Mary wrote to his mother as follows:

'Dear Madam and worthy Mother, —You have heard from your holy and much loved son that the full weight of the cross is on us, and that we must consent to reverence as a Bishop him whom we loved and venerated as a priest. Here at La Delivrande all hearts are full, and many tears have fallen, but we are brave before our good Father, that we may not pain him. The world has nothing except compliments and felicitations for you with respect to an event which reflects honour on all your family. For me, I congratulate you on being the mother of an apostle of Jesus Christ, and on the heavenly favours which he will draw down upon all belonging to him. But my greatest wish is to suffer with you, and sympathise in the grief of your heart, and of those who feel as you do. I thank God for the grace given to you, that his father should see only the gilding of the Cross in the raising of his son to the episcopate.

'The consecration will take place on the 26th of October, when we hope to receive all the members of his family. You must make a great effort to come, in order that he may see many round him. His Lordship is no prouder than was thc simple priest who sought only to hide his virtues and sufferings. His titles and honours weigh heavily on him, and if anything could alleviate our sorrow, it would be the tribute of praise which all render to his virtue and merit.

'My good mother, pray that God may come to our aid after withdrawing our guide and stay. You will always find in poor Mother St. Mary a heart that understand you. Permit me to take his place as far as possible, and to be henceforth the confidant of your sorrows, difficulties, and troubles. To find a friendly heart which can share in them will be a relief to you, and will give you an opportunity of assuaging my sufferings in return'.

To divert her own thoughts, the Reverend Mother busied herself in the preparations necessary for receiving the Bishop of Bayeux, and twenty French priests who came to pay their tribute of respect to Dr. Vesque. A dormitory in the still unfinished building was partitioned off for the priests, the Bishop was lodged in the nun's refectory and children's day school, while the Sisters took their meals by turns on the shelves in the linen room.

The chaplain of Norwood would never be persuaded to accept any retribution for his labours, and so had nothing wherewith to provide the vestments requisite for his new position. The community, glad of having the opportunity of making some little return for his services, worked night and day to prepare all that he could want, Mother St. Mary thanking each particular Sister as if for some personal benefit.

After his consecration, Dr. Vesque was summoned to Honfleur; his mother, who was believed to be dying, had entreated him to come and give her the last blessing. He passed a few days with his family, and his mother having partially recovered, returned to prepare for his journey to Rome, before leaving for his diocese.

About this time one of the religious was declared to be in the last stage of consumption. Though of high rank and promising talent, Mother St. Stephen passed a hidden life of piety and usefulness. She occupied much of her time in mending the kitchen linen, and at her death so complete was her spirit of poverty, that not even a little picture could be found belonging to her to send to her friends. While employed as organist and teacher of music, it was only obedience that compelled her to show the talent which she really possessed. Dr. Vesque thus wrote of her: 'You know what she was, her love of poverty, mortification, and common life, her exceeding simplicity, and let me specially add her love of silence. My dear children –and I speak to the religious– she had been rich, she was of a delicate constitution; in the world she might have led a very different life, here she was unknown and unthought of. How much mental power, how much true wisdom is there in this! Follow in her footsteps, and the gifts which God has bestowed on you will be a thousand times more fruitful for His glory and for the salvation of souls. Dear orphans, you loved Mother St. Stephen; she used to teach you singing. You little know what zeal she had in her work. But you will, I hope, often pray for her. Which of you will undertake the care of her grave? You are aware I do not like rank weeds in the cemetery. I used to go there sometimes and pick up the weeds I found. You will go there now, and do this for me, and say a *De Profundis* for those whose bodies lie there.'

One of the first ideas of Dr. Vesque after his consecration was the project of a foundation in Dominica of a house of the Institute of the Faithful Virgin, and it was agreed with Mother St. Mary before his departure that he would make preparations for a little colony which was to follow as soon as he was ready to receive them.

On January, 1, 1857, Mother St. Mary assembled all the religious in her room, and thus addressed them: 'Here is my new year's wish to you all, my dear daughters, that each one may be a bond of union and charity in the house. Choose one day in each week for self examination on this point, and see whether you have made any advance; but if, instead of being a promoter of charity, you find you have wounded it, make a firm resolution that you will during the succeeding week redouble the practices of meekness and sincere charity. You are all good children, and you wish to be united in charity, and if you write to me that you are daughters of obedience, I shall know that you have accomplished that charge. Remember, my daughters, it was the last word of your good Father here on this very spot. If we have but one mind and one heart God will refuse us nothing. The year we begin is an important one, for a year of election and I hope a new foundation must be important. Above all, be women of faith. Let nothing human, nothing natural, enter into your views. Pray to God to guide you to make choice of those whom it is His will that you should elect, and as to the foundation of Dominica, pray that He may govern the hearts and minds of those chosen to be sent to that much needed work. No impatient desires, no attachment to one place rather than another. Let each have her heart ready for all, saying often to God, "Lord, what wilt Thou have me to do". It seems as if God had taken our Father from us here in order that some of us might labour for the salvation of the little ones in America.

'Be persuaded it is not enough to say that we will what God wills, and that we work for Him. Remember we can work for God only by sacrificing ourselves. It was to save souls that Jesus Christ became a little child, that He waited nine months in His Mother's womb, that He suffered privations and poverty unto the death of the Cross. And it is by suffering in every way that we shall do His work. Oh, my dearest children, after God has tried us as He has done, after He has taken from us, one after another, those who seemed destined to be our support; when He has imposed such great sacrifices on us, how can we refuse Him lighter ones? How can we now be attached to our own will, or be put out by some mere trifle? We were accustomed, my children, to find in Father Vesque the true guidance of the Holy Spirit; we knew we had but to shut our eyes and follow blindly the wisdom of his direction; we saw God only through him. Now God wills that we should go to Him first, and so we must pray more earnestly and recur to Him in our difficulties and doubts with all confidence. We have none but Him to look to, and so He will refuse us nothing.

'The spirit of charity which binds La Delivrande to Norwood must unite us with those who go to Dominica; the distance is greater, but no matter. It will be our younger sister, and in families the young ones are always petted. I tell you with joy how consoled my heart is when I see what the Sisters of La Delivrande have done for Norwood, the sacrifices they make for the building here, suffering voluntary privations, and imposing sacrifices on themselves; they really have one heart and one soul with Norwood. May that spirit always remain amongst you. If all our houses are thus united, if all the Sisters have that sweet affable charity that now reigns between you, there will be nothing that you cannot obtain from Almighty God.'

A few days later the little chapel was decorated in its most festive array for an interesting ceremony. The newly consecrated Bishop received the abjuration of a young lady who wished to be admitted into the Church by him, because he had in the beginning of his labours at Norwood received her brother, to whom she was tenderly attached, and whom the chaplain held in high esteem during the short period that the young man lived after becoming a Catholic. An orphan also, of the age of thirteen, brought up a Protestant, and unbaptized, received the grace of conversion when witnessing the baptism just conferred. This poor child, had felt convinced in her own mind since April, 1856, but foresaw such a future of suffering if she embraced the truth that her courage failed, and she had not dared to take the final step. But two days before the departure of the Bishop, she gave herself fully up, and was baptized and confirmed by him. Great was his joy at being thus allowed to offer one of his orphans to God before leaving them for ever, and at the end of the ceremony he exclaimed: 'My dear children, look upon this soul in its angelic purity as the last gift of your father, and as a sacred treasure which he confides to you. She is the fruit of your own prayers and sacrifices.' On March 17, 1857, the final separation between the Father and his children took place, and

Mother St. Mary lost the guide who for nearly nine years had been her consoler and director. She returned to La Delivrande on April 4, 1857, to make everything ready for the day of election. Each department was visited in detail and put in order, her last advice was given to each one of her daughters, her directions for the plan of education completed and delivered, and then with grateful satisfaction she prepared to lay down the charge of Superior General, which she had again held for six years of suffering and trial.

Chapter XVII

Mother St. Mary Superior of Norwood. Opening of the New House. Departure of the Missionary Sisters for Roseau, Dominica.

On May 23, 1857, Mother St. Remi was elected Superior General, and the house of Norwood had the happiness of receiving Mother St. Mary during the short time that yet remained before her death.

But if her return was a subject of rejoicing to the religious of Norwood, it was not without deep regret that those of the mother house received her farewell, and the blessing which proved to be the last.

Dr. Grant, amongst others, welcomed her on her return, for he thus wrote to her:

'Reverend Mother Superior, —After an absence of six years you return to Norwood, and you will not fail to bring with you the same desire to make the work prosper which you showed at its commencement.

'The children, in their grief, will be consoled that the Immaculate Virgin restores to them their first Mother of Norwood, and I hope their piety will prove to you how grateful they are to God for giving you to them at the moment that this new house, the fruit and the memorial of the generous sacrifices of La Delivrande, will demand of you the fresh sacrifices that a new foundation always requires of the superiors and religious. I bless the result of this election, and requesting the prayers of your Sisters, I have the honour to be,' &c.

Passing through London, Mother St. Mary stopped at St. George's to receive the Bishop's blessing. 'Ah', said he, alluding to the new house, 'you are come to make a new foundation?' 'Yes, my lord'. 'Then there must be a death'. The mother Assistant remarked that an orphan was very ill. 'Oh, that will not do; it must be a religious'. How soon were the words to apply to her whom they hoped to preserve for many years yet!

We need not say with what pleasure she was received at Norwood to be, in the words of the children, 'our own Mother'. But she refused to take any party in the management of the house during the five days that elapsed before her official recognition according to the ceremonial of the Institute, and even reprehended the Sisters who applied to her.

On the 5th of June, after her installation, she addressed her religious as follows: 'We must consider ourselves as about to begin a new foundation, since we are about to occupy the new house and to receive a greater number of children. We must, so to speak, be steeped in the religious spirit, and all personal wishes and desires, all little passions must be entirely set aside. Bear towards each other the same charity which is felt for you at La Delivrande, where each religious deprives herself of something for her English Sisters. Be all of one mind. You will have many sacrifices to make in order to acquire this spirit. But if, instead of wounding or irritating a Sister when fatigued, you help her, another day she will do as much for you. Mother and children all must work for one end. Pray for me and do not throw a cloak over my defects. Remember that those in charge will have a special account to render of the example which they give to others. Love God with all your hearts, with that generous love that leads you to do all for His greater glory. Let us be all the more united from feeling our late loss so deeply.'

As though she foresaw that her life was hastening to its close, she was now more zealous to advance the perfection of her religious than she had ever been before. She entered into the minutest details, and that no time might be lost, the work to be done in the week was assigned to each office, and those to be employed in it were chosen by herself conjointly with the first Mistress of the Orphans. All was foreseen and provided for, and when once the arrangements were made, she did not allow them to be altered unless it was absolutely necessary.

The annual retreat followed shortly after her arrival. 'Make a good retreat, my dear children', she said, 'and this it will be if it makes you more supernatural. Come to God with all your imperfections and often say to Him as an ejaculation: "Lord take away, and then give to me. Take away my little passions, my self-will, everything in short that is not according to Thy Heart, and give to me the love of Thee and the virtues that ought to adorn my soul to make it agreeable to Thee." Forget your employments, forget everything, that you may think only of God and of your soul, and be alone with Him.' When she perceived that God required a painful sacrifice of a Sister, she tried to incline her will to it, and lead her to wish to do what He willed, by proposing motives of faith; and when she found her disposition generous, she would redouble her kindness. On the other hand, if she met with nuns who showed negligence in doing what was prescribed, she suffered greatly, and has been known to perform herself practises of humiliation when these were omitted by some of the Sisters. 'My children,' she often said, 'never defer your penances, there is nothing so opposed to a religious spirit, for it is by them that your Divine Spouse wishes you to expiate the faults which have perchance saddened His Heart. Besides which, this penance properly performed might perhaps have merited for one of our children the grace to resist some temptation, and at the last day you will be astonished to see how much her fall may have been occasioned by your want of generosity.' She never appeared wearied by the importunity or by the defects of her religious, nor was she ever disheartened by delay. There is an instance of her waiting nine years before pointing out a slight defect to a Sister. Mother St. Anne (de Valori) felt a particular attachment to a prayer book which had belonged to her deceased daughter. The good Mother allowed her to retain it for several years, till after a retreat Mother St. Anne of her own will gave it up. 'I knew you liked it too much, but God had not asked of you yet to give it up for His sake,' was the remark of Mother St. Mary. The most imperfect of her daughters seemed to have an especial place in her affection, and she had the art of inspiring in them a filial confidence in herself, while she always listened patiently to whatever they had to say, as though she had nothing else to do.

Towards the end of June, Mgr. Vesque made a formal application to the two Bishops, and to the Superiors of the Congregation of the Faithful Virgin, for the foundation of a Convent in Dominica. All readily responded to his appeal, but Mother St. Mary feared lest some of her daughters might be actuated in the matter by motives of natural affection rather than of zeal for the salvation of souls. She therefore assembled them and spoke to them in detail of the privations those who went would have to undergo, privations both spiritual and temporal, the frequent absence and perhaps the death of their holy Bishop, the poverty of their community, and of the island, the fevers and diseases so frequent in those tropical regions, past habits of long standing to be broken through, and others to be adopted. In fact she omitted nothing calculated to test the true character of their enthusiasm, but at the same time she appealed to their faith by pointing out the abandoned condition of the children and the number of little souls to be saved, and she communicated to her religious the ardour which consumed her own breast for the cause of so many poor orphans. She concluded by telling all to recollect themselves before God, to weigh their strength, and only to undertake going abroad if they felt themselves equal to the privations attendant on the step. After a solemn invocation of the Holy Spirit, the votes were collected and found to be unanimously in favour of accepting the mission to which they were invited. The good Mother's countenance was now radiant with joy. 'Well you are good children. I was right to tell the Bishop that he might depend upon you, and that you had not degenerated since Norwood was founded. He will rejoice to hear his children are disposed to become as mothers to the little negresses of the West Indies as well as to the orphans of England.'

She would have been delighted to go herself, but sacrificed that wish to the greater good of the Institute, and made up for it by preparing her children, telling them how often she had longed to work in foreign missions for the extension of God's glory. 'We are making,' she said, 'a novena in order to learn whom God selects for the work. Give yourselves entirely to Him, let those who remain humble themselves, and those who go be full of confidence. In the name of God, my daughters, I entreat you to give yourselves wholly to Him, that He may take or leave you here as He likes. Do you think our Lord did not suffer when He accepted the chalice of His Passion? Die, if it needs be by obedience, even if you die in the ship going out. It is obedience that robs Hell of its prey. No doubt you have to abandon everything, but when you are chosen by Holy Church for such an apostolate who could refuse it? Offer yourselves to God in your Communion, promise Him to go to the antipodes if obedience sends you. It is the work of saints. How could we hesitate when God chooses us who are so unworthy. To fight against Protestantism, to labour for the poor negroes, to clothe the naked. I can allow but one feeling to my daughters—that of regret on the part of those who remain in Europe. Listen to the words of Jesus Christ: I thirst for the salvation of souls, I thirst for thy heart, I thirst to see thee a faithful spouse. Those whom God selects for the mission of the Antilles will be martyrs of charity and devotedness. The Lord will know and welcome them at the last day. It is a great mark of predestination to be thus called to a complete sacrifice. But those who remain will also work for their Sisters by offering up their actions in their behalf. Let us all then strive to become saints, my dear children, and accustom ourselves to suffer, so that we may completely belong to God.'

One morning Mother St. Mary, reading in the soul of a particular Sister what effort it cost her to make an offering of herself for Roseau, went up and placed before her an open book wherein an answer was given to all her difficulties and doubts. The astonished religious could only thank God for having made known her temptation to her.

In the meantime the new building was nearly finished, and on the 10th of July, after distributing the rewards and decorations to the children, she singled out fifty as especially distinguished for good conduct, and giving to them the name of the 'privileged class', sent them to live in the part of the new house destined for them. We may here give some account of her manner of forming the lady boarders to whom she uniformly showed the affection and interest of a mother. Her principle was to appeal to their sentiments of piety, honour, and good feeling. She put before them the influence which they were called upon to exercise on society, especially on English Catholics, the danger, on the one side, of injuring their faith through contact with heresy, or of frightening from Catholicism well-disposed but timid souls by an ill-judged or exaggerated manner. The frank, open avowal of their Catholic convictions, their superiority to human respect, and their watchfulness over the tendency to self-indulgence, so common at the present day, were carefully inculcated. She used to recommend cheerfulness as a double duty. 'Let Protestants remark your happiness in your faith, and they will wish to share it with you.'

She very seldom scolded; a friendly observation or an appeal to their sense of duty was the usual reprimand. The young ladies have often declared that she seemed to know their faults by intuition. Thus, for instance, when some had laid a plan that at their French recreation they would be irreproachably polite, but were to say nothing, she went to meet them the moment it was finished, remarking in a kind tone: 'How is it, my dear children, that you have been so well behaved at recreation, and yet have not been speaking? With a little goodwill you could soon express yourselves in French, but you will never be able to do so till you try, this however you can do more easily and pleasantly here than when you go back to your families.'

One day a Mistress had acted with indiscretion, and the pupils had retaliated by making themselves as disagreeable as possible. Mother St. Mary came up and after sending the obnoxious Mistress away for a few minutes, asked them if in the world they would not often meet with people with whom they could not get on so easily; and she then proceeded to show them the necessity of overcoming their first feelings, pointing out that real virtue requires us to be particularly kind to those whom we are least inclined to favour. She asked them as an act of reparation to behave well on the following day, a promise which was gladly given, and faithfully carried out. At a period when she was most overwhelmed with occupation, she found time to come day after day to visit the boarding school and encourage three little sisters, of the ages of seven, nine and ten, who were just beginning to sew and make dolls' clothes. One would have thought, to see the interest she took in the matter, that she attached as much importance to the doll's dress as the merest child would, but by the time that it was finished the children had learnt how to sew.

No one knew better than the Reverend Mother how to make exceptions without compromising authority, thus she could take the part of one who seemed to be unjustly or over severely reproved, or could make a compassionate excuse for an unhappily constituted disposition. Again she told her religious: 'Be no afraid to say to a pupil: "I will not reprove or punish you *now*, because my temper might be too hot;" and do not fear that the children will think you unjust if, taking account of the fiery or irascible nature of a particular child, you pass over some faults, when you see that she is really trying to overcome herself.'

Early in August, 1857, serious difficulties arose with regard to the foundation at Roseau; however, the good Mother was encouraged by Dr. Grant to persevere in her intention. 'I have myself,' wrote the Bishop, 'opposed a foundation about to be made by religious, and found it very hard to overcome the repugnance which I felt to the scheme; nevertheless when undertaken it seemed to succeed well. Saints say that the foundations to which people in general take exception present no very wonderful history, since the world does not desire what is good in any way, but that those foundations turn out to be the greatest and richest in fruit, which pious persons dislike at the beginning. Pray unceasingly that the Immaculate Virgin may be the Mother of Dominica, as she has been of La Delivrande and Norwood, and the thorns will not fail to bear flowers.

(Signed) T. Grant.'

The Sovereign Pontiff also sent a special benediction on the enterprise; Mother St. Mary had applied for this through Mgr. Talbot. At the foot of their petition the Holy Father wrote with his own hand—

Romae apud S. Petrum, die 17 Sept., 1857. Benedicat vos Deus, et custodiat vos in via, ut cum pace salute et gaudio revertamini ad propria.

Pius P.P. IX.

'May God bless and keep you in the way, that in peace, safety, and joy, you may arrive at your true home.'

In the middle of August, 1857, the Superior General came on a visit to Norwood. Mother St. Mary wished to make this an occasion of inculcating on her daughters by example the respect and profound deference due to the Mother placed at the head of their Institute. She superintended the preparations for her reception, placing in her room all the little objects of devotion which she knew she liked. She had written to the Mother General for authority to incur some extra expense. As no answer came the matter was left undecided. The Assistant told her that she should presume leave, as she was sure Mother General would approve. 'No,' replied Mother St. Mary, 'I have no orders from Mother General.' On her arrival the latter seemed both surprised and displeased that she had not followed the advice given, as the nature of her answer might have been taken for granted. Thus Mother St. Mary was able to practise humility and obedience at the same time.

The ceremony of the opening of the new house was fixed for September 24, 1857, and the good Mother looked forward to this with much pleasure, but it seemed that for her no event could come without its cloud. On the eve of the day appointed the news reached her of the sudden death of her only sister the Countess de Jumilhac, an especial benefactress of the Convent.

Mother St. Mary assembled her daughters round her on the vigil of the feast of All Saints, and after an earnest exhortation to union, charity, and a life of faith and sacrifice, followed by the solemn invocation of the Holy Spirit, she named, on the part of Mother General, who had returned to France a few days previously, the Sisters destined for the new mission in the island of Dominica, of whom two were from La Delivrande, and four from Norwood. One of the orphans was to accompany them as portress, and their departure was fixed for the 2nd of November, and the Reverend Mother herself took care to see that everything was prepared and packed up. The books they had at Norwood and their stock of music were divided into two parts, one being intended for Roseau. She seemed to have a presentiment that this farewell was for eternity, and could at the last moment utter only a few parting words. 'Never forget,' she said, 'the benediction you have received from the Holy Father. Be one in heart with La Delivrande and Norwood, and with each other.' Dr. Grant himself accompanied the Sisters to the station, and after their safe arrival at Havre, where they were joined by the two sisters from La Delivrande, they sailed thence for their destination in Dominica.

We pass over the many events of a thirty days' voyage to quote from the letter of Mgr. Vesque which announced the arrival of the missionary Sisters in the *Occidental*, a fine sailing vessel. 'Rejoice with us,' writes the Bishop, 'your daughters arrived last night. They landed at Martinique at one o'clock this morning, and now at half-past nine they are getting up and preparing to breakfast. Yesterday as I visited the work at the Convent I cast my eyes over the sea, and saw a sail on the horizon. I concluded that it was the *Occidental*, but the glass showed me only one of the schooners that ply between Martinique and Guadaloupe.[1] On going to rest I remembered that Dr. Grant used to say nuns always like to torment the Bishop, and I thought to myself, now our Sisters will arrive during the night. Nor was I far wrong. My first glance this morning pleased me much. The corridor has been changed into a dormitory furnished with two beds, three sofas, and mattresses on the floor. My parlour shall be the community room; as to the refectory we must see later on. These provisional arrangements remind me of Sydenham Grove. We miss you very much. Pray God your spirit, and above all His Spirit, may be with us. The Sisters have settled down very satisfactorily. They will describe to you their new life here, which is not like anything they have before seen or anticipated. But it has not begun yet. When I think of all they have to get through in a month!... I make them exercise that activity, without dissipation and without fuss, which I so much wish for in religious. I should like to give them a better reception, but I cannot. They will remain here a month. I will take care they do not lose the religious spirit. In a month we shall have a boarding-school, then we will undertake the "free schools." This evening the Sisters will teach Catechism, and on Sunday will superintend the children at Mass. Poor good Mother! I am so happy to have your Sisters. There is in your community so much zeal, obedience, and silence. May God bless you again and again.'

Although the difficulties and privations encountered in the commencement of the work at Roseau do not properly belong to this life, yet they were so personally connected with Mother St. Mary and with Mgr. Vesque, and so strongly marked with the traits of their spiritual character, that the details given in the following letter deserve insertion, were it only for the interesting picture which they present of the real hardships borne by nuns in a foreign mission.

'Every morning the Bishop comes to give an explanatory lecture on the organization of the schools, in parallel groups of benches and desks. He is so

[1] The religious were actually on board this vessel, as the *Occidental* had disembarked them at Martinique, and they could get no other ship to take them to their destination.

good as to point out to us what seems really to the advantage of the children, as also what we need not attach any particular importance to. His principle always is "few words."

'To complete the furnishing of the new Convent, what we want particularly here are things which speak to the eye. We have at present nothing of the sort, and every object of this kind is too costly for us to purchase. We have not even a single picture or image of the Blessed Virgin, or any one thing to mark the religious character of the house.'

In another letter we find the following description: 'The ceremony of our installation took place on January 20, 1858, the feast of the Faithful Virgin. As we left the gallery to go to our oratory we found Monseigneur in the parlour, where he gave us a little exhortation, which made us all cry, and the good Father himself, saint though he be, cried too, and did not try to hide it. He bade us join him in saying the *Miserere* and the *De Profundis*, and then proceeded to say Mass, the chapel being so full that we had to kneel out in the corridor with three young people who wish to become nuns. On this occasion the Bishop pillaged his own room most unmercifully in our behalf. He laid his nicest books on the table of our parlour; his candlesticks, his vases, and his crucifix contributed to ornament our chapel, and finally he looked out all his little pictures, and made us paste them on some kind of cloth, leaving a margin for a frame. This was done in order that every Sister might have a picture of the Blessed Virgin, of her guardian angel, and of St. Joseph in her room. It was quite useless to say anything or to make difficulties. His plate, his glasses, all were put in requisition, and you may picture to your own mind how bare he left himself. He told us before how he suffered to see us take possession of so poor a house, without even seats to sit down on. In vain have we told him that we were quite happy; it so upset him that it was enough to make us all feel ill. As there were no tables in the refectory we placed two window shutters on a wooden tressle, and sat on our boxes. The flooring is only earth, with here and there a few paving-stones, which seem as if they were afraid to join company.

On this feast day a little Carib orphan, between five and six years old, entered the Convent, and received the name of Marie Fidéle; and very soon the nuns had fourteen more children consigned to them. Twenty-two pupils came daily to receive an European education. Then a school of boys was placed under their direction, and soon the charge of one hundred and eighty girls was added. Joined to this they had the supervision of the sacristy belonging to the cathedral, which had been neglected for years; they had many children to catechize, many people to instruct and prepare for confession and Easter Communion, and retreats to give for first Communions. All these details present a very insufficient picture of the apostolic and laborious life of the daughters of Mother St. Mary. She, on her part, never ceased to load them with proofs of her affection, and never let an opportunity escape of sending them out large boxes filled with whatever she thought they wanted.

In April one of her daughters wrote to acknowledge the receipt of a package sent out by her. 'We have just received your grand packing-case, my dear good Mother, and oh! How happy you have made us. If you could have seen our joy as we looked over all the things, and thought of the care with which you had collected them, you would have been quite rewarded by the mere sight of the unpacking. When Monseigneur saw what was in the little box which contained everything necessary for the sacristan, he had it sent to me, that I might have the pleasure myself of unpacking it, and soon joined us himself to partake our joy. Have you had a revelation of what we wanted? If you had been here you could not have chosen better.' It is painful to reflect that this letter came too late to be read by the spiritual mother to whom it was addressed.

The Holy Father, through Monsignor Talbot, not only again sent to Mother St. Mary his special benediction, but also promised to confer upon the convent at Norwood the relics of one of the youthful martyrs of the early Church, taken from the Catacombs. To this unknown virgin martyr the Pope gave the name of Innocentia, with the desire of placing the innocence of the children under her special protection; and when it arrived on January 23, 1858, the much-prized relic was borne in solemn precession to the chapel. The Saint's body was afterwards placed by the Reverend Mother in the principal class-room, to be, as she said, 'first mistress,' and subsequently it was carried to the infirmary to watch over the sick, when several orphans were cured through the Saint's intercession. Relying on much past kindness shown to them, the children wrote and asked Father Faber to compose a hymn in honour of St. Innocentia. The following was his answer to their request.

ST. INNOCENTIA

Dear little Saint, sweet Innocence.
Thy throne in Heaven we see,
Jesus, thy love, the eternal King,
Hath done great things for thee.

Our own dear Saint; make us like thee,
Be thou our kind defence;
Give us thy gift of modesty,
Sweet Sister Innocence!

In days of darkness, when the world
Despised our saviour's name,
Thy childish heart, by grace grown old,

Gloried in such dear shame.
The Roman children knew thee well,
Light-hearted in thy play,
Filling the vineyards with thy songs,
The gayest of the gay.

They saw thee at thy daily tasks,
Obedient, gentle still,
They learned from thee how softly love
Its duties can fulfil.

They wondered at thy modesty,
Thy soul's most sweet defence;
It made thee like a queen to them,
Dear little Innocence.

And now thou art a real queen
Up in the land of Heaven,
Jesus to thee a jewelled crown
And fadeless palm hath given.

In grand old Rome thy love was set
On our dear Lord alone;
He saw the secret of thy heart,
And took thee for His own.

He loved thee midst the orange trees
And flower-beds of thy home,
And mid the Sunday worshippers
In the close catacomb.

He loved to hear thee sing the songs
The Christian songs that tell
Of the Good Shepherd, and the sheep
That Shepherd loved so well.

He made thee grave, and all the while
He made thee grow more gay;
Thy heart grew lighter through the weight
Of love that in it lay.

He gave thee faith that made thy heart

Strong as the walls of Rome!
He gave thee love and purity,
And then He called thee home.

Dear martyr child, they tore thy flesh,
With fire they scorched each limb;
The sword then gave the final stroke,
How sweet to die for Him!

And now thou art with Him, fair child,
Nestling at His dear feet;
Thou knewest that Heaven was bright, but not
That it was half so sweet.

Mother St. Mary had the satisfaction at this period of procuring regular work for the children, a want which must be experienced to be fully understood. They were employed in needlework by contract as far as their lessons and the various household offices permitted. When her health prevented her from going amongst them she used to send for the best behaved to her room, and conversed affectionately with them, mingling advice with anecdote. Many a long task has been finished, many a hard lesson learnt, many a little difficulty surmounted by the thought of 'going to our good Mother's room'.

Ever intent on what could contribute to the wellbeing of her little flock, she saw with concern that in bad weather their only place of recreation was a dark wide passage at the foot of the stairs, where gas had to be used in broad daylight, and where the space was too confined for the children to play with freedom. She begged penny by penny the money required to erect a playroom for them, and her collection was still very far from sufficient when a legacy left by her sister to the orphans enabled her to put a large iron building where they could more freely enjoy themselves.

Additional room made it easy to give speedy admission to a considerable number of children, a gain which was not without its dangers and difficulties. Fully sensible of these, Mother St. Mary one day remarked: 'I acknowledge, my daughters, that it is an anxious time, to have such a number of new children to receive, while so many things have to be arranged, but then this gives us an occasion of practising great virtue, and of winning a look of love from Jesus. Each one of you who passes through and surmounts these difficulties with energy will draw down the most precious gifts on the community. Labour to make yourselves worthy of what I promised in your name to our Holy Father, that when we should be numerous enough we would be ready to go wherever he sent us, all over the world. How happy should we be if one day he deigned to look on us. It would then indeed be God waiting to shower

His graces on us. Tell me, my children, if I have promised too much to Christ's Vicar on earth when I answered for your devotedness to God's glory? I trust not.

'Raise your heart from time to time to God', said she to a religious who felt fatigued after spending a long day in taking charge of some troublesome children, 'rest in the heart of Jesus Christ, and place your children there with you. He says nothing, but He looks down and smiles with love on your efforts to keep them free from faults.'

To another lamenting her incapacity she replied: 'Yes, doubtless you would be incapable of this act without obedience; so much the better that you see your own inability; but faith obtains all things, and you will obtain what you desire from Almighty God if you go to Him with confidence.' And she added with a smile, 'to win over Almighty God by your confidence is to attack Him on His weak side.' A religious having asked her how to obtain missionary zeal, she replied: 'Faith alone can fill the heart with that spirit. If we do not feel its impulse we must humble ourselves, pray much, and offer ourselves to God each day in sacrifice, that He may do what He likes with us, notwithstanding our repugnance. Oh, my children, with what different eyes we shall see things in the other world. Let us ask ourselves each day what we shall wish to have done at the hour of death, and let us be blindly obedient in carrying this out in the smallest details.'

It was considered extremely desirable to obtain possession, if possible, of a certain field adjoining the Convent ground. Many efforts had been made in vain, the ground belonged to a college, and was inalienable. However, one of the youngest orphans buried a medal of St. Germaine Cousin under a tree in the field, and the affair was intrusted to the shepherdess, who had lately been canonized; the field was known in the convent as St. Germaine's field. During the Reverend Mother's life no attempts met with any success, but immediately after her death the obstacles were removed, and the field being advertised for sale was purchased by the Convent. The religious attributed this successful issue to the intercession of their venerated Foundress.

On the occasion of a visit from Dr. Grant during the last month of this year, 1857, to hear the confessions of the religious for the jubilee, Mother St. Mary placed herself very unreservedly under his Lordship's spiritual direction, and continued this confidence in him to the last.

A charitable association had been formed in England in 1853 for the purpose of maintaining a larger number of children. In 1858, thanks to the zealous efforts of a devoted friend of the house, this good work attained a much greater development, and the following pious custom, since carefully continued, was then established. The names of all those who contributed twenty pounds were inscribed in the list of perpetual subscribers at the door of the church, and it was decided that on the first day every month the Holy

Sacrifice of the Mass, and a general Communion of the religious should be offered up for their intentions, the orphans attending at the Mass, and praying specially for their benefactors.

When, in February, 1858, Cardinal Wiseman, accompanied by several friends, paid a visit to his dear children of Norwood, a lady who accompanied his Eminence was much struck with the unfavourable change which had taken place in Mother St. Mary's appearance, and earnestly begged permission to send her own medical attendant for a consultation. The good Mother expressed great disinclination to see a stranger, and the religious, accustomed to witness her painful sufferings, could not persuade themselves that there was any especial cause for uneasiness, so that no step was taken at the time.

The Reverend Mother having especial cause for great anxiety in a matter that affected the well-being of her community, directed the children to make a fervent novena to St. Innocentia, that it might be averted. One Sister having asked permission to offer herself as a victim of charity for the same intention, the Reverend Mother declining the offer, said, 'Our little saint shall herself choose the victim.' A few days later she told the same Sister, 'St. Innocentia has chosen her victim, and she has not made choice of you.' The words produced but slight impression at the time, but when shortly afterwards the good Mother herself was seized, the opinion gained ground that she had made an offering of herself in order to obtain the favour so anxiously solicited. In one of her letters to Dr. Grant at the time she says: 'Our dear children were most edifying on this occasion, I made them pray very hard, without of course telling them why. They spent one after the other a whole hour in inward adoration, during which for the smallest fault they asked a penance from their mistress. A miracle was required, and they obtained it by the help of our little St. Innocentia; I seem to waken from a painful dream. May God be for ever blessed.' But the great mental anxiety which she underwent during this short time had a fatal effect on her health, already so much impaired. She again lost her voice, and seemed to think her end was not far distant.

A part of the community still inhabited the old house, and the Reverend Mother had an extreme dislike to change into the new one, where all the disposable space was occupied by the boarders or orphans, without much convenience for religious observances. She had even arranged matters so as to remain as long as possible in her room, but the Father Superior having decided that she ought to go to the new house, because the regularity of their life suffered through the necessity of passing from one house to the other, she sacrificed her own repugnance that she might render immediate obedience. The same evening she removed into it with so much apparent satisfaction that those of the Sisters who did not know her so intimately imagined she was especially pleased with the change. Her room was situated in the centre of the house, where she heard all the noise made by the children; yet her particular regret was that her room should be so large, whereas the Sisters were put to very great inconvenience. The movements of the children and the echo coming from the wide and lofty staircase did, in fact, occasion an amount of suffering which, in spite of her efforts at concealment, could not escape the anxious watchfulness of her daughters, and they entreated her to return to her former quarters; this, however, she declined doing, for she considered it her duty to remain.

As long as she was unable to use her voice she wrote in the class-room, and during the morning, when the children went to clean and sweep the different parts of the house, she made herself useful by standing on the stairs to watch them as they passed. Her mere presence inspired them with the spirit of exactitude and carefulness. She herself regarded, and she wished her religious to regard, each little new-comer as a soul snatched from the grasp of the enemy, and brought to them by God Himself to keep. 'Little children', as she remarked, 'remember for a whole lifetime the first reception they meet with. Be kind to those who are strange and distressed in mind. Be always and everywhere motherly. When you have difficulties with the children, picture to yourself Jesus on the Cross before you, and unite each pain you feel to His. He will carry your cross for you if you work for Him. Duties accomplished in the midst of consolation have already their reward, but those that are fulfilled in desolation and bitterness will have a double recompense. Smile at what annoys you, for all to which you naturally feel dislike will be rewarded in Heaven. I would wish to make the children the main object of your life. You ought to be so happy to be near them. Try to make a child like that which you want her to do, by this means you make her both happy in herself and ready to love you.'

In the month of March an affcction of the eyes obliged her to have her room darkened, but as she had recovered her speech she thanked her Divine Master for not depriving her of two organs at once. Her voice returned after she had made a novena to St. Philip Neri, Father Dalgairns having sent her a picture of the Saint, to which a relic was attached. In the beginning of April a considerable improvement took place in her health, yet at recreation she often spoke of her death as approaching. Seeing her increased anxiety in instructing and forming them, the religious might perhaps have anticipated the blow that was impending over them, but they did not admit the possibility of it into their minds.

Chapter XVIII

Last illness, Death, and Funeral of Mother St. Mary. Letters of Condolence.

The following sentences from the pen of a Sister who describes the events before the death of Mother St. Mary, will show how much the eyes of all were closed against the perception of any immediate danger.

'For thirty years the heart of our beloved Mother had beat but for her children, and even now they were the object of her thoughts. Her hours of suffering were passed in asking an account of the class, of each child in particular, examining their clothing, cutting it out by means of measures which she could feel, so as not to fatigue her eyes, while some verses of Holy Scripture or the Imitation were read to her from time to time. Holy Week was for her a season of suffering, and Easter brought her no joy but that of union with her crucified Saviour. Towards Low Sunday she felt better, and said, smiling, "I thought death was at my heals, but he seems to have turned aside." Yet the anticipation of death seldom left her. On lying down she often said, "I shall perhaps never rise." At other times she remarked, "I feel life ebbing; I have but one regret, poor children, you will be so sad. You need me yet. ...But what pride is this?... God needs no one... When I am gone all will go on well. When in Heaven I will watch over all the houses, and will go from one to the other. Travelling there above is rapid. I will stir you up, I will warn you. I will show this one that she is not charitable, that one that she does not look sharp enough after the children, and if you don't attend... Beware!." She also remarked, "I think I have lived long enough. God will call me suddenly; you will let me die without the sacraments, without even my crucifix." This she said even when a slight improvement allowed her to press on the work she wished to finish.

'All these signs of coming change should have awakened our anxiety, but they did not. We had been too much accustomed to see her suffer; one day ill and the next at the head again of the community. She had so often spoken to us of her death as of the moment when her happiness would begin. How could we believe her last hour so near. "It is impossible," said we. "My children, you will see it will soon be over." The doctor had warned us years before that the gout might prove fatal in a few minutes; but we trusted to the Faithful Virgin who had so often restored her to us, almost from the grave, and we forgot that the fruit might be ripe and the reward ready.

'On the 23rd of April she spoke even more than usual of her approaching death. Her whole afternoon was spent in a new arrangement of the dormitories. She went to them herself, helped to push the beds into their places, and make up each child's parcel and when their bedtime had come she remained to preside over them, attending especially to the little ones, and earnestly blessing them when she left. It was not till half-past nine that she went to supper and to rest.

'For some time she had denied herself a particular kind of nourishment which suited her, but which she did not consider necessary. "Well," she said, "I have not made a vow to take no more. I am tired; give me some now." The next day she directed the placing of the tables in the nun's refectory, and regulated some matters connected with serving. On the last Sunday of her life she attended High Mass; the Gospel was a development of the words, "A little while and ye shall not see me."

'At the usual hour she went to the class-room to read out the weekly notes, and distribute the decorations. She decided some points of detail into which she had not yet entered, and appeared in good spirits on leaving the class. "I have got through a great deal this week," she remarked; "If all I have arranged is carried out, things will go well." She drew up the notes of the work to be executed during the following week, and gave one to each Sister written with her own hand.

'Monday the 26th she passed in putting her correspondence straight, and finished this occupation by writing a note to the Superior General concerning an orphan. It was the last time she was ever to use a pen. She was present at the recreation of the community, and went out about two o'clock for exercise, taking the longest walk she had done for some time. She had a little difficulty in walking, but persevered resolutely as a duty. She spoke of taking the best behaved of the little ones with her in future, as a means of giving them more encouragement. During her walk she again mentioned her death as being near, expressing her conviction that she would never see again those absent ones who were dear to her. It was evident she wished to give as much effect as possible to each action, and so spent considerable time in visiting the various offices, such as the dairy, the wash-house, the ironing-room, the kitchen, and the refectories. She stopped to encourage the children whom she met, and to make observations to the religious, appearing much pleased. Thence she went to the carpenter's shop, and spoke kindly to the workman who declared that the precious advice she then gave him would be remembered to his dying day. On returning to her room she dictated a letter on business, and asked for a list of the children. As it was not quite the usual hour for this it was not ready, and she herself went to the class for it, as though fearing she might not have time. The mistresses felt surprise at this unusual haste, but the list was brought, the rewards given, and she blessed the children for the last time, returning afterwards to her room. After taking supper as usual she complained of being unwell, and retired to bed. Up to ten o'clock her feeling of indisposition increased, but presented no very remarkable symptoms. She sent the Mother Assistant to bed, saying she hoped to sleep, and did in fact dose for a short time. At four on Tuesday morning she felt worse, suffering from violent headache and from acute pain in the side. "My child," she said to a religious, "pray for me," and on her assuring her that she did, she added, "Oh, yes! pray that I may do God's holy will, as the saints and angels do it in Heaven." The doctor was summoned, and mustard was applied without effect, the pain increasing, and the breathing becoming affected. Prayers were now said for her in thc house, and two Masses were offered up.

'The doctor declared her malady to be acute rheumatic fever, which would probably last for several months. He prescribed medicine, but refused to bleed her, assuring us that the patient was so weak the loss of a very small quantity of blood might be fatal. He saw her three times that day, and on his second visit changed his opinion, and said the attack was pleurisy along with gout, though danger was not immediate, and he attributed the illness to a chill, which, however, the good Mother had not perceived. She inquired what he had said, asked to make her confession, and begged Father Morel to allow her to confess daily, as she might be called away very suddenly. During the day she remarked, "I shall lie two or three days panting like this, and then it will be all finished." When told that was impossible, she replied, "My poor child, you will see." She inquired in the evening who was to pass the night with her, Mother Assistant answered, "I, of course." Mother St. Dosithea also begged to remain. "Oh, you are good daughters, I know it is hard on you, and I had sacrificed in my own mind the satisfaction of having you with me." She made Mother St. Dosithea lie down repeatedly, and tenderly inquired if Mother Assistant had rested. Touched with their anxious desire to afford relief, she said, "God bless you, poor children, I give you so much trouble." On the third visit, at eleven in the evening, the doctor said: "She is no better, but she is not worse, and that is a great deal." He tried other remedies. The patient remained in the same state till three. The pain was acute and the oppression very severe. The remedies applied produced no effect. The night was spent in loving colloquies with her suffering Lord, Whom she invoked by His bitter Passion, His painful scourging, His shameful death on the Cross, His adorable Body, and precious Blood. She had great devotion to these petitions, adding the words: "In this painful distress, Lord deliver me," or again, "O Jesus, be a Saviour to me;" "Faithful Virgin, protect me," and other pious aspirations. On Wednesday morning Mother Assistant and Mother St. Dosithea perceived a rapid change for the worse; the pain amounted to agony, the breathing was laboured and painful. Three messages were despatched for the doctor.

'We wished to have a physician from London, but there was no train. The next idea was to send a man on horseback, but the horse was lame. The patient warned her daughters that she felt the sense of suffocation increasing, and desired everything to be prepared for receiving Extreme Unction. We wished to wait for the doctor, but she replied with calmness, "My poor children, believe me, I am in my last agony; you will let me die without sacraments. Listen, do you not hear the death-rattle?" She sent again to hurry Father Morel. On coming he said to her, "You ask pardon of God for all the sins of your past life?" "Oh, yes, Father," she said, "with my whole heart." He then gave her the last rites of the Church. The religious who were assembled round her could not restrain their sobs. "Why are you so distressed?" she said, in a tone of gentle reproach. Some of the Sisters went to prostrate themselves before the Tabernacle, entreating God to spare their beloved Mother, and once more asking the Faithful Virgin to restore her. Our rule directs that before receiving the viaticum a religious shall ask pardon of her Sisters, and renew her vows; but the prescribed formula would have been too long for her, as the utterance of each word was a very painful effort. While the priest went to bring the Blessed Sacrament Mother St. Mary raised her voice, and in the gentle tones so well known to us, said: "My daughters, I ask your pardon for all that I have ever caused you to suffer, and for the omission of much good that I might have done you." The Mother Assistant answered in the name of all that it was her daughters who begged her to forgive them, and then, taking her hand, kissed it. The good Mother pressed it affectionately against her daughter's lips, replying, "Yes, my daughters, I pardon you with all my heart." On the return of the priest she was able to receive the holy viaticum, though with some difficulty. The doctor at last arrived, and when she heard him announced she asked for her veil, which had been removed to relieve her oppression. Her daughters hesitated; "Good Mother, the state you are in dispenses you." "No, no, our veil; the rule, my children, the rule!" "Madam," said the physician, "you are very ill." "Yes, sir, I am dying." He added aside to the Mother Assistant, "It is all over; the gout has risen, and when it touches the heart she will expire." As the Mother Assistant repeated for her the words, "Father, into Thy hands I commit my spirit. Jesus! Mary! Joseph! a slight movement of assent passed from her lips, and after gently sighing three times, her lips quivered a little, and she calmly expired.'

Mother St. Mary died on the morning of Wednesday, April 28, 1858, at the age of fifty-six years, of which she had spent twenty-seven and nearly four months in religion. Her daughters, as they knelt round her bed, and gazed on the placid features, could not realize that she was dead. The first impulse of the Mother Assistant was to invite all to ask their beloved Mother pardon for every suffering they had occasioned her, to renew their religious vows, and promise to be all of one heart and one soul, as their Foundress had so often recommended.

The poor orphans at first refused to believe in her death. 'We have prayed so much and with such faith and confidence', they said; 'how is it God has not heard us? Whilst her body remained at Norwood, all asked permission to watch and pray by the side of it, and could scarcely be persuaded to leave. Her hands and feet were covered with tears, and they crowded round to touch her with their rosaries and medals.

The doctor, speaking of her last illness, remarked that she was one of those persons whose indomitable courage scarcely admits of the progress of disease being observed. It is evident that she must have suffered intensely during her whole life, from the extreme delicacy of her constitution, which was acutely sensitive to an attack of pain that in other persons might have been comparatively trifling. A capacity for suffering seems one of the special gifts conferred on holy souls, as a trait of resemblance to their Divine Master, Whose adorable Body was formed to endure such exquisite agony.

The instant after she had expired, Dr. Grant entered the house. He was himself so ill, that the effort to move at all was very great for him, but he had managed to get as far as Norwood, in the hope of arriving in time to impart the last blessing. The holy Bishop prayed long by the side of her mortal remains, and then endeavoured to console her daughters, mingling at the same time his tears with theirs.

A telegram announced the sad news to Father Rivière at Caen, where he met the Mother General on her way to Norwood, having still hopes that she might find Mother St. Mary alive. After telling her of the fatal result, and bidding her hasten to Norwood, which she could only reach on the following Friday, he himself carried the intelligence to La Delivrande. The children were summoned to the chapel for Mass, and the Father Superior, as he passed from the sacristy in black vestments, merely uttered the words, 'My children!' His tone of voice indicated the rest, and turning round after Mass, he said, 'I think you have all understood, my children, that you are doubly orphans, and that your good Mother is no more.'

When told that Mother St. Mary was not to be buried at Norwood, Bishop Grant inquired whether her heart at least might not remain with them. 'My Lord,' replied the Mother Assistant, 'our good Mother always said to us, "My body I leave in the hands of my Superiors, they will do with this as they please after my death, but I particularly wish that it should not be submitted to any medical examination."' The spirit of this request was respected, and thus Norwood was deprived of the desired privilege.

Night and day the religious succeeded each other in watching and praying around their beloved Mother, who had been to the end their guide and model. Though she could no longer speak to them, every heart felt her influence still present with them. No one experienced the painful gloom and depression usually caused by the sight of the dead, but the soul of each was filled with that calm sorrow, which checked all tears, and bade them not to mourn as those who have no hope, but, on the contrary, as those who are fully assured their Mother would still watch over them, and not leave them orphans.

The children asked to have their names written and laid upon her breast, and all, at the solemn service celebrated next day by the Bishop, offered up their Holy Communion for her soul. Ill as he was, Dr. Grant made three journeys between Norwood and London that day, in order that everything might be arranged for sending across the venerated remains to the motherhouse. The Mother General arrived a few minutes before they were deposited in the leaden coffin, and could therefore once more see the kindly features, and kiss the cold hand, so dear to her. The orphans took their places in dead silence, some tried to kiss her again, and the youngest caressed her feet with their little hands.

On the coffin were inscribed the three words 'La Delivrande, Norwood, Roseau,' expressing a brief but eloquent epitome of her whole life. The bed on which she had expired was changed into an altar for the Confraternity in behalf of the souls in Purgatory, and the mourning decorations were left on it for a year. It was a loved resort for her daughters, where they meditated on her life, her instructions, and her death. The following account of her funeral is condensed from a paper published at the time:

'The remains were expected to arrive at Caen on Saturday, and many preparations were made for the reception of one who had been so universally beloved and admired.

'The Bishop of Bayeux had ordered that, in the event of their arrival on Saturday, a Requiem Mass should be celebrated in the Church of the Hospital of St. Louis, and all the clergy of the town and neighbourhood were to accompany her from Caen to La Delivrande.

'Part of these arrangements could not be carried out, as the stormy weather prevented the arrival of the body till the following day. A large number of priests and friends were waiting on the quay at Caen. At their head were the Father Superior (Vicar-General of Bayeux), the former Father Superior, who had for many years been the help and guide of the late Reverend Mother, and the reverend chaplain of the motherhouse. The parochial duties of Sunday prevented most of the priests who were present at the landing from accompanying the remains to La Delivrande; a party of ladies and friends, however, rendered this token of affection to the departed, leaving Caen about one o'clock.

'Meanwhile the community at the motherhouse were preparing for this last sad arrival, so different from former visits, when joyful and happy faces greeted her. Now every heart was full of sorrow; but feeling anxious that their beloved Mother should once more receive some token of their affection, a deputation of seventy-two of the orphans, accompanied by forty of the boarders, wearing white veils, and carrying lighted tapers, went two miles along the road to meet the funeral cortège. They were joined by a numerous procession from the villages, the inhabitants of which mournfully took their places round the bier of their former benefactress.

'In passing before the Chapel of La Delivrande, the procession paused. The coffin was deposited for a few moments at the entrance, the large bell was tolled, and a *Libera* was sung in full choir by the mission priests belonging to the chapel, who joined the procession from thence to the Convent, singing the *Miserere*.

'At the first sound of the bell, the younger orphans and boarders came from the Convent to meet the procession. The crowd at this time was so dense that fears were entertained of the procession not being able to reach the cloister, but the greatest order prevailed. The religious were assembled in the choir, awaiting the arrival of the body of their beloved Foundress, which was preceded by Madame de Montpinson, the Superior of the Hospital of St. Louis, and by the Countess d'Osseville, aunt of the deceased. The Office of the Dead was chanted by the clergy and community, after which the assistants retired, to meet again on the following morning. From that moment the religious and orphans by turns watched and prayed unceasingly near the remains. At nine on the following day the clergy and relatives and friends of the Reverend Mother again assembled for the last service. The chapel was thronged, and a Requiem Mass was sung by the Father Superior, who could scarcely overcome his emotion, and whose voice faltered when he came to the words of the *Pater, "Fiat voluntas tua*." After Mass a few words of eulogium were spoken by the Father Superior, who alluding to the incident of the poor assisted by Tabitha, claiming her restoration to life from St. Peter, added that in the case of the Reverend Mother St. Mary, it was not only garments for the body that might be shown to our Blessed Lord as the gifts of her charity, but that spiritual clothing, which she had prepared for the souls of the orphans by the Catholic education given them in the three establishments which she had founded.

His lordship having granted general permission for all who had assisted to enter the enclosure, a procession was formed. First came a hundred and thirty of the orphans, preceded by the banner of the Faithful Virgin, then followed the boarders and nuns, the cross being carried before the clergy, who walked in front of the coffin, while a vast number of relatives and friends came last, amongst whom were to be seen many orphans formerly belonging to the house, now drawn together to testify their love and gratitude by their presence.

Arriving at the cemetery, enclosed within the grounds of the Convent, they deposited their beloved Mother in a modest grave towards the centre, surrounded by her religious daughters and orphans. No earthly distinction marks her resting place, but the gratitude and heartfelt affection of all those to whom her life has been devoted will ever make it to them a hallowed spot. When all but the relatives of the late Foundress had retired, the Count de Jumilhac and his sister, the Countess d'Iquelon, visited the poor orphans, and in a most tender manner entreated the children to look upon them as their future protectors, and to concentrate on them all their affections as the last branches of a family which had always loved the orphans so much, assuring them, at the same time, that they on their part would ever preserve for them the affection of their beloved aunt.

A few simple words from a letter written by the orphans of La Delivrande to Norwood will show the good work she had done in their souls, and the depth and tenderness of their personal love for her. 'When our good Mother came to the class and said, "My children, I have just received a telegram from Norwood, Mother St. Mary is dying; they say there is no hope; go quick and pray at La Delivrande," we consoled ourselves by saying, "Oh, yes; we will pray for her, and then the Blessed Virgin will give her back to us. But, alas, it was too late. She was no longer in this world. If they could but have told us sooner we are sure we should have been heard. We found our Mother and Mother St. Aloysius Gonzaga crying bitterly at the feet of the Blessed Virgin; we knelt by her and prayed so hard, we felt sure we had been heard. Our good Mother left for Norwood, and we went and worked all day in dead silence, praying every hour to the Blessed Virgin and St. Innocentia. About eleven o'clock we saw Father Superior come, and everybody went to the chapel. Oh, he did not need to tell us any more; our poor hearts understood it all. There was nothing but sighs and sobbing to be heard. We never felt such grief. We could not follow the Mass, we were crying so. Oh, yes; we were right to regret her. Her only thought was for us; she lived for us. All her happiness was in her little children. We loved her and will never forget her. When we took her to the last resting place, we went shedding bitter tears. No one could feel such terrible grief as ours. When we are tempted to do anything we think, "Will Mother St. Mary be pleased?" and if we think not, we don't do it. When we want anything from our good God, we always go to our good Mother first, and we are sure to get it. It is our great reward to go to her tomb, and we don't forget our Mothers of Norwood there. ...'

Dr. Grant's letter to La Delivrande contains the following passage: 'God, Who knows what the love of such a Mother is, spared your feelings by breaking at one stroke the ties which it would have been much more painful to sever one by one.' Our Lord does not forbid tears; He accepts them as a tribute of affection and gratitude; but He asks of you not to be down-hearted, to practise faithfully all the instructions given you by your Mother; for every time you will be obedient to her recommendations, to the spirit she tried to inculcate, you will give her the consolation which perhaps you may not always have procured her whilst she was on earth. Oh, be strong and courageous! Imitate the greatness of that soul that knew so well how to join energy to virtue, courage to piety. She confides you now to Mary Immaculate, to God, Who will always be your Father. Stay with Mary at the foot of the Cross; she will be your and your orphans' Mother, and Mother St. Mary will herself watch over you.'

On the Sunday following, his Lordship celebrated High Mass at Norwood, and preaching to the faithful on the text taken from the Gospel of the day, 'It is expedient for you that I go away,' after some beautiful reflections on the necessity of suffering, he added words which may be read in memoriam, not of one only, but of both of those who have passed away from us: 'If the parish must always be united to the community, it must be more so than ever after the loss they have just experienced in the Reverend Mother Superior, whose life offers a model of all religious virtues. She consecrated her existence to the relief of the orphans; she wore out her strength and consumed her life in the practice of zeal for God's glory, a zeal which, when she saw that glory compromised, made her pray and weep until God had shown mercy to those who were about to outrage His goodness. Who can tell how much she suffered! God took from her all those dear to her. Those who guided her in the task she had undertaken. Some left her; God sent others into distant lands, and death took from her those who were the object of her most legitimate affections. Amidst these trials no murmur ever escaped her lips. She understood God's ways with His elect. She continued alone the work she had begun, and loved to the end those who had inflicted sufferings on her. Such is the love of God. She loved those who did not respond to her benefits, and, like Jesus, it was the poor who were the objects of her tenderness. Let the religious who so justly lament her be consoled; the dead speak from their graves; she will always speak to them. Like the saviour of men, she will tell them from Heaven what she could not say on earth. Ah, when God removes our guides in the path of virtue, let us not be disheartened or lose confidence. He will send His consoling Spirit, Who will teach us what we could not learn before, and will do more for us than we had dared to hope. God alone changes not; and when He bestows on us a gift full of His Spirit, let us not murmur when He resumes it, for He reserves other favours if we are faithful to profit by the cross He sends us in His love.

'Pray for this soul which God placed amongst you a model of charity; help to raise her to the full possession of that happiness which will be the reward of her long sufferings. Seek to win a crown beside her whose days were full before the Lord, and make her example live again amongst you. He is the Father of the orphan and the broken-hearted. He left His Mother fifteen years alone on earth, and He said to His Apostles, "It is expedient for you that I go away."

Cardinal Wiseman came to Norwood on the 6th of May, and assembling the orphans and religious, addressed them in words full of affectionate condolence. 'Formerly it was your holy Superior and beloved Mother who welcomed my arrival; she whose presence spread happiness around her. Until now, my dear children, your joyous faces met me with smiles, and I found you busily occupied, while your merry songs were echoing the happy feelings of your hearts. Today I am struck with the grief depicted on your features, so opposed to that gaiety natural to this season of the year. I know, my children, the affliction you have had. You have experienced an irreparable loss; you weep for one who can never be replaced. How shall I console you? If I speak of the great virtues of the dear Mother you have lost, I shall make your scarcely dried tears flow afresh. Dear children, it was this good Mother who had assembled you all here, poor orphans, so early deprived of your parents; you owe her everything. ...How many little ones has she not relieved! This heart so large, so full of the love of God and the poor, nourished the little seed she had sown, until it grew into a large and beautiful establishment.

'And you, my dear Sisters, I would fain pour some drops of consolation into your hearts, resigned and yet crushed by the loss you have sustained. These little children cannot yet understand *that the hand that smites is the hand that heals, and that the hand that casts down also raises up*. You have received a blow that one might call mortal, and perhaps at the first moment of your grief you were tempted to think that it was the ruin of all your hopes, and that all you had done under the powerful guidance of your Mother was about to crumble to pieces. You found not around you either the virtue or the strength necessary to continue this great work. But after the first moments of desolation your faith awoke, and you perceived that after all your Mother had taught you she still had another example to give. She had shown you the religious life in all its perfection. Her presence alone was an instruction in virtue. Her words sweetened your trials. Her advice guided you, and you rested at her feet like a child in the arms of a prudent mother. There was yet another lesson to teach. She had to show you how to die in the practice of your vow to the orphans, and in the observance of the rule. She had taught you how to live for orphans, she has now shown you how to die for them. Had she been too anxious in taking the precautions which her wretched state of health might seem to justify, she would have been surrounded with a thousand little indulgences which you would have readily conceded, and still considered her an example of virtue. But no, to her last hour she laboured, toiled, and wore out her strength; careless of herself, she had no thought, no life but for her children. By her last words she enforced the love of the rule in the house which she had founded. Her love was all for God, and in Him for all the souls that He had confided to her. You have then learnt a last lesson in that holy death, and now your thoughts must be for Heaven. You know where your Mother and Foundress is; she has not left you, she still holds the place in which you loved to see her. She is amidst you, or better still, above you, among the guardian angels of your children; but, like them, she does not echo our lamentations, because, absorbed in the joy of her Lord, there is for her no more suffering... . God saw that her work was already founded. Yes, I declare it to be founded, and that nothing will overthrow it; for it was a part of the character of her we regret that what she did was done solidly. God gave her a large mind and generous soul; He will form on her spirit those who succeed her in the work so well begun. God saw that she had accomplished the task He had imposed, and He has judged that it was time to remove her, in order that others might give proofs of their love, their piety, and their wisdom. Then do you labour to imitate her, and I promise you in God's name that the work will prosper, and of all the good done by the hands of those that succeed her it will be said, "It is the benediction of Mother St. Mary that still hovers over you, and falls like refreshing dew on the house she has founded."'

The virtues of Mother St. Mary had thoroughly gained over the sympathies of one who had keenly opposed her while at Bayeux, but who now wrote: 'I partake in the sentiments of profound respect, affection, and admiration which your letter expresses for the venerated, I had almost said saintly, Foundress whom you regret. What a beautiful soul! What ardent zeal for God's glory! What thirst for the salvation of souls! What universal charity! What humility united to so much courage, and such brilliant qualities of mind and heart! How much good she has done, and how great will be her reward! I hope she already enjoys it; for God had purified her in this world by all manner of sufferings, trials, and crosses. I shall not the less remember her at Mass every day of my life, hoping she will sometimes remember me before the Lord.'

The Bishop of Roseau was pained at the suddenness with which he heard of the Reverend Mother's death. He writes: 'Yesterday Dr. Lynch opened his letters, and told me, as a piece of news which might perhaps interest me, that the religious of Norwood had lost their Superioress... . This intelligence made my heart very sad at St. Thomas', for it was there that I learnt the new misfortune that had struck me. Blessed be God; blessed for ever be His name! However hard His will may seem, it is the will of a kind Father. No, I will not complain; I am ready to suffer; may my sufferings shorten the time of expiation which our imperfections may have caused that good Mother; may my sufferings be agreeable to my good Master, and obtain some consolation for you. I cannot console you; I know too well what you have lost, and what I lose. I can only entreat you, dear Mothers and daughters, to grant me one request. The body is nothing, the soul is all man. The bodily frame of your good Mother was too weak for her fervent heart, God has removed it from our eyes, but it was not that which loved religious perfection, and delighted in the holy asceticism of the rule. Her body was too weak and feebly constituted to labour so constantly for the education and instruction of our dear children, for the religious, the novices, the boarders, and orphans. It was the energy of her will that sustained her delicate frame in spite of itself, and had mercy on it only when it was utterly exhausted. It was the energy of her will that accomplished the smallest details of the law, and suffered for God's work, and which made her reproach herself incessantly for the indulgences imposed at times by necessity. Well, dear children, it is the spirit of your Mother that I conjure you never to allow to die out from amongst you. Think not of bringing her body back from the grave; we need it not; but we need her spirit, and it depends on us to keep it from ever dying in our regard. May it live in each of us, and then we shall be consoled. We cannot but trust that our Mother is in Heaven, that she prays for and protects us. We will rejoice in her happiness, and provided we preserve alive her spirit, her works will remain. It is for us to fulfil the sacred trust which she has confided to us. I would like you to view her as always amongst you, with one hand offering you the rule and her instructions for the education of children, as though she said "Behold your Mother," while with the other hand she shows you her orphans, saying, "Behold your children." Then, when we meet her in Heaven, we shall be able to tell her, "Mother, we have been faithful to the maternal rule you gave us; we have loved, respected, and obeyed it. Behold, too, the children which you left to us, to be your crown and our own."'

Before he had heard of Mother St. Mary's death, a letter from the Bishop contained words which read like a presage of her death: 'You will see the death of the Bishop of Martinique. I would not speak of it in my letter to our Mother. ...Alas, I tremble... . *I do not know in what state these lines will find you.'*

A celebrated barrister (M. Bardont), whose motherless daughters had been carefully educated by her, writes: 'Ah, what have we heard! She who received in so many families the well-merited title of "Our Mother" is no more! Permit me to mingle my tears with yours. I feel more bitterly than ever the loss we have all sustained in the death of this holy Foundress. When I saw so many members of her family taken away, I had hoped that she would be spared to us, and to her good work, which was always widening, the circle of those personally attached to her. But, alas, it was not to be so! She was ripe for Heaven, and the death of Madame de Jumilhac was but the prelude to her own. What she has sown in tears will not perish. ... But how much grief and regret she leaves among all those who knew that great and noble life too soon concluded.'

Mgr Vesque (1817-1858), chapelain du couvent de la Vierge Fidèle à Norwood, puis évêque de Roseau

Mgr. Vesque (1817-1858)
Chaplain of the Convent of Our Lady of Fidelity
at Norwood, and Bishop of Roseau.

Couvent de la Vierge Fidèle fondé à Roseau,
capitale de la Dominique, en 1857

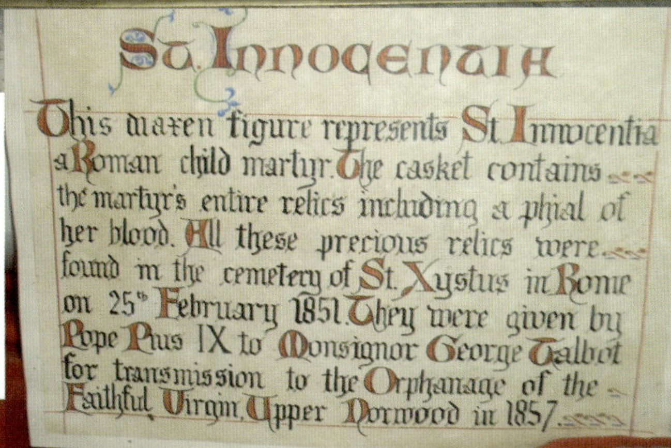
St. Innocentia
This waxen figure represents St. Innocentia a Roman child martyr. The casket contains the martyr's entire relics including a phial of her blood. All these precious relics were found in the cemetery of St. Xystus in Rome on 25th February 1851. They were given by Pope Pius IX to Monsignor George Talbot for transmission to the Orphanage of the Faithful Virgin, Upper Norwood in 1857.

Mother St. Mary's room is now the school chapel

Mother St. Mary's things

Cross worn by Our Rev. Mother St. Mary

Chapter XIX

Virtues and spiritual directions of Mother St. Mary; her Faith, Charity, Prudence, Humility.

The extracts which we have already given from some of Mother St. Mary's letters and instructions, together with the incidents narrated in the course of her life, will doubtless have already given the reader considerable insight into the main points of her spiritual character, but the lesson and example of her life as a whole would be insufficiently described were we not to follow the usual custom by dwelling upon her virtues in detail. Of these we naturally place at the head the spirit of faith which directed her in every thing she said or did, and shed a heavenly light upon her view and appreciation of each thing that happened to her. ' I care little,' she remarked, 'for the judgments of men, if at the Last Day the Sovereign Judge of all approves my actions.' When consulted she used to remain lost for a moment in recollection, then with gentle firmness gave her answer. If it caused displeasure she frequently replied: 'I may be mistaken, but I sought God's will, which is all I care for.' 'We should at once place ourselves at the disposal of God's will,' was one of her maxims, 'so that whenever any good work undertaken by us is interrupted or prevented by the course of His providence, it ought to require but five minutes recollection in God to obtain our perfect resignation to all that may happen to us. Let us put aside our own views and opinions, that we may be clothed with the spirit of our future life, and live as religious in the light of eternity. When in trouble let us say: "This comes from God, Amen," or when assailed by difficulties, "God wills this. Fiat." Let us constantly compare the few days of this life with the length of eternity. The supernatural life teaches us to receive everything as from the hands of God, and to do everything for Him alone. It is to the want of this spirit that we must attribute all our faults, for without it how can we bear interior trials, or struggle against our own nature; hence the wounds which we inflict upon charity, hence the pride by which we so often sin against others. The supernatural life alone enables us to see Jesus Christ in our Superiors, whom we ought to obey as representing God to us, and to acknowledge in every equal a Sister whom we are bound to love and assist to the utmost of our ability. Nothing but a life of true faith can support us in difficulties, or reconcile us to crosses and contradictions, as being conducive to our real happiness. To attain this we must endeavour to make a complete oblation of ourselves, saying at each new sacrifice of our wills: "I desire, O Jesus, to do everything which thou willest." To do what God wills, and as He wills; to suffer what He wills, because He wills it, that is the secret of all sanctity. Be with God like little children, holding their mother's hand and taking no thought whither she is leading them; trust in God as a child does its mother, and be docile children in His hands. Throw yourselves into the arms of the ever-faithful Virgin, and be assured she will not reject you from her, nor let you fall.'

Jesus Christ dwelling in the Blessed Sacrament was her counsellor in all her doubts; and her first impulse under the pressure of any difficulty was to throw herself at the feet of our Lord, seeking for light and strength from Him. She endeavoured to persuade her daughters always to seek the same help. 'Go,' said she to a Sister who was oppressed by some heavy trial, 'place your doubts and fears, and even your repugnance in the Sacred Heart, and do not rise until you feel that a glance of love from your Divine Spouse has restored calm to your soul.' It was remarked that whenever she gave an order to her religious she prayed for its success, so that the faith of the Superior and the obedience of the subject really worked wonders. To prevent the perpetration of a sin no sacrifice appeared to her too great, and more than once she was heard to say, in the fullest conviction of its truth, that if the foundation of Norwood prevented but one sin being committed, it would have repaid all that had been bestowed on it. Any negligence which exposed a child to the danger of sinning at once raised her indignation, though no other fault seemed capable of doing so.

The jealousy with which Mother St. Mary watched over every point connected with the supernatural life obtained for her the grace of a most childlike confidence in God. She spoke to Him with ingenuous simplicity and abandoned herself entirely to His providence in the most critical circumstances, with the strongest assurance that sooner or later she would find everything turn out to her own greater good and to His honour and glory. She bore each obstacle and difficulty without losing any of the peace of her soul, and used to say: 'Let us bide God's time, for He is faithful and will not fail us.' Again, when one of her religious was disheartened, she answered her: 'Take courage, this is for you the time of struggle. But let your motto be "always against nature." All suffering will have a term; go then bravely forward, and be simple and open with your good God. Speak to Him as to your best friend. Seek God in sacrifice, and you are sure to find Him; when tempted do a little more, if you wish to surmount the difficulties that come in your way. Come and ask a blessing from your Mother, and say with confidence: "I can do all things through Him that strengthens me." ' She showed by example, as well as by word, that a soul which entirely confides in the direction supplied for her by God will make rapid progress in virtue, and that it is only by our fidelity and generosity in overcoming ourselves that we merit God's especial graces. Her correspondence is full of notes or letters of encouragement to her spiritual daughters, in which she always bade them look up to Heaven as their goal, to have nothing to do with sadness, but to fly its very first attacks as an open-mouthed dragon ready to devour them, remembering that aridity and temptation is a time in which to make a great step forward. The weaker they felt themselves to be, the more, as she assured them, would God clothe them with His strength, if only they would have confidence in Him. They should see in Him a loving Father, choose what would most please Him, and if they did not feel themselves strong enough to make a sacrifice required of them, they were to tell Him so in all humility and simplicity. In all this we see the reflection of her own mind, as trained by God's grace.

The love of God was the great moving principle of Mother St. Mary's life. Her favourite beatitude was: 'Blessed are the poor in heart, for they shall see God.' The festival of the year which she most loved was Christmas Day, and she exhorted her whole community to prepare for it in a special manner, bidding them contemplate with all love and confidence the Infant Jesus. She had a singular gift in leading souls to serve God from motives of love, rather than of fear, and to work with a holy joy and a hearty goodwill. When a sacrifice came in their way, she would have them consider their Heavenly Spouse, thirsting to gain souls and looking to them to help Him. When an intimate friend, Madame de Bourmont, once showed her a relic of the true Cross, she at once, though in a very suffering state, knelt down and prayed for some time with such deep earnestness and devotion that her companion, impressed by her manner, knelt beside her and begged of God to grant to her the same grace that she saw her friend petitioning for with such fervour. When they both rose, she mentioned to Mother St. Mary what she had done, when the other replied with a smile: 'You will perhaps have more than you bargained for, since I was begging that our Lord would inspire me with the love of the Cross, and then lay upon me as many crosses as He chose.' If Mother St. Mary loved God with all the warmth of her generous heart and sought every means of proving this to Him, her love of her neighbour was not less remarkable. Like the beloved disciple, she was continually repeating the words: 'My dear children, love one another,' for she never ceased to recommend earnestly the most perfect union and practical charity between the different houses of the Institute. Her own actions were unfailingly directed by these maxims, which were ever in her mouth and heart. 'Remember, you must sacrifice yourself for the advantage of others; you must suffer in order to do charity. Give all you can and expect nothing in return; accept from others all that they make you suffer, but see that you impose no suffering on them.' Thus when one of the religious spoke with some asperity about an orphanage established in opposition to theirs, the holy Foundress exclaimed, with much energy: 'Oh! my children, how grieved I should be, if I thought you were jealous. Rather rejoice that other communities do good, and let there be no spirit of rivalry amongst us. You must have no desire to monopolize the good works of God, or I would disclaim you for my daughters.' She would never allow a painful impression to remain in the mind of another after she had been obliged to refuse anything, and her gentle hand always softened the pain occasioned by a reprimand. She owned that it was one of her greatest crosses to have to say or do anything which would grieve another; and she was ingenious in contriving ways and means of consoling and encouraging those with whom she had been obliged to find fault.

Under another head of charity, she wished to obtain for those towards whom she herself acted in such a spirit of charity, that same consideration at the hands of the Sisters in religion. She at once attributed to God's permission, or to His actual providing for them, any pain or annoyances caused them by fellow religious. 'It is not always,' she would say, 'the imperfections or defects of our Sisters that are trials and mortifications to us, God often makes use of their very excellencies and virtues to be as goads and incentives to stir us up, and spur us on. Let us suppose a particular Sister is irritated and vexed at the slowness of her companion in office, yet it is equally true that her companion is suffering as much, very possibly more, from her undue vivacity and natural restlessness of manner. In what family have the members been the occasion of keener suffering to each other, than were Jesus, Mary, and Joseph in the Holy Family itself? Consider the painful misunderstanding that took place between our Lady and St. Joseph, yet she spoke not a word in explanation. Then, in that act by which Jesus stayed behind in the Temple, what agony He inflicted on His Blessed Mother, yet there could be neither in Him, nor in it, the shadow of imperfection. Let each one, like our Divine Lord, go through life doing good to others, and making herself an imperceptible bond of union and peace in the community. The more antipathies and dislikes we conquer, so much the more holy shall we become. When we render a service to our Sisters, the eye of God dwells on us with complacency. Remember it is a precept, not a counsel, to return good for evil; never complain, but be happy that you have something to bear, not forgetting that she who is the first to humble herself will carry away the crown. Let each one after intercourse with her Sisters frequently ask herself whether she has left them pleased, and has been to them what she would like them to be to her. Happy the religious who covers adroitly the defects of her Sisters, excusing them both to herself and others. What we suffer from others is often the best means of correcting our faults, and supplies the best antidote to our self-satisfaction.' The purity of her own charity and spiritual affection for her daughters in religion is clearly indicated in the care with which she directed to God as its centre and motive the legitimate affection felt so strongly towards her by all in the community. Thus she would say that she had no objection to their filial love and confidence in her, looking upon her as the channel of their union with God in religion, and finding strength and consolation in the words addressed by her to them in His name.

But she most distinctly warned them against the attraction of mere human affection, which would destroy all her power of being of any real use to them.

Mother St. Mary was not less remarkable for her prudence than for the virtue of charity. That which she decided as really for God's glory she carried into execution with rare intelligence, and she also knew how to put the right person in the right place. She selected for each one the employment best suited to her capacity and disposition; and, far more than this, she elicited hidden powers of usefulness in Sisters who as little knew as their immediate Superiors often did, what they were really capable of doing. When her duty led her to speak to the community she carefully weighed her expressions and waited for a favourable opportunity of introducing any particular subject. She never had to accuse herself of speaking too strongly, even in her intercourse with persons living in the world, for with singular tact and ready sympathy she was able to identify herself with the interests of private families, and yet hurt the feelings of no one. She possessed another quality most necessary for the work to which God had called her, the maintenance, namely, of strict justice and impartiality. This each individual orphan soon discovered and knew how to appreciate, placing the utmost confidence in the equity of her decisions, and feeling sure of a gentle reception and patient hearing from one whom they all loved and trusted as a mother.

With her naturally courageous, earnest, and lively disposition, the subjection of the religious life, especially under the circumstances in which hers began, must have been a somewhat stern and abrupt master in the school of humility. The bodily infirmities of her youth were to Mother St. Mary a source of very constant and painful humiliation, and that at an age and in a position of life in which she would have been expected to shine, more especially when we consider her natural character and endowments. Besides this, Father Saulet subjected her from the very first to a trying spiritual discipline, and took every opportunity of planting the seeds of humility deeply in her soul. Yet she never showed the slightest inclination to revolt against the sternness of his treatment; her only rejoinder being: 'God knows the truth, and that is enough for me.'

One day, having received a Sister rather stiffly, she knelt down before those who had been witnesses of her manner, and asked their pardon for the bad example which she considered she had given.

Her condescension towards her daughters often excited their admiration. Once, for instance, when she made an observation at the recreation, a Sister thoughtlessly said: 'Oh, Mother, don't say that,' and the Foundress with utmost amiability replied: 'Well, I will not say it again.' Her humility, far from being ostentatious, was most carefully concealed. She used to call this virtue the key of God's treasures, saying that if a soul came before Him without it, she could not hope to receive any of His heavenly gifts, and would go away poor and empty-handed. Above all she recommended that solid humility which loves to be unknown and to be treated with contempt which before God she acknowledges that she deserves.

'Sound the depths of corruption in your hearts,' she would say, 'and be not surprised to find a swarm of acts of meanness there. The more of our faults we consent to see, the more God will reveal to us. When we have been guilty of a fault, let us rise again with courage, deepen our conviction of our own nothingness, and trust still more in God. Sometimes we deceive ourselves, we make a comparatively easy sacrifice in one way, and seek compensation for this, on some other point, by allowing ourselves little self-indulgences. When we see and are persuaded of our own nothingness God shows that He is thinking of us and comes to our assistance, but when we trust in ourselves He leaves us to ourselves.

'If we acknowledge our faults generously before men, God will often excuse us, even when men condemn us. Ask often for the grace to know yourself, and remember we can do all things if we have but humility and confidence in God. I want to see in you generous hearts that refuse nothing to grace, and that make their faults conduce to their greater humility.'

Chapter XX

Mother St. Mary's observance of the vows of religion. Her devotion to our Lady. The vow of the care of orphans.

The desire of imitating our Blessed Lord having led Mother St. Mary to leave her family and the possession of riches that she might be poor like Jesus Christ, she not only had a singular love of poverty herself, but most carefully instilled the same love into the hearts of her daughters, both by word and by example. She taught them to regard themselves as the servants of the poor, ever carefully and assiduously working for them. She insisted that everything which was used should bear the stamp of the most rigorous poverty. The furniture of her own room was the simplest possible, comprising only objects of absolute necessity, made of the commonest material; and, distrusting the habits of her early life, she eagerly sought lessons of thrift, questioning the Sisters as to how matters were managed most economically at home. She was as narrowly on the watch against the slightest waste as she was generous and liberal in her charities. During the winter of 1841 her father sent her a warm short cloak, well lined. She asked Father Saulet if she might put it on when she had a cold, but he made her give it up in his presence to another religious, and desired the latter to use it. Since her infirmities prevented her wearing a dress made of as heavy a stuff as the rest, it was proposed that she should use one of light merino instead, but this she firmly refused, saying that her title of Foundress bound her, more even than others, to a literal observance of the rule.

She never permitted her daughters to consider anything as belonging to themselves personally, not to make anything to serve their own private convenience. More than one piece of work undertaken without the sanction of obedience was condemned to be burnt by the delinquent's own hands. And notwithstanding her zeal for the decoration of the church, she would not allow some flowers to be placed on the altar which were obtained in a way that she considered an infringement of poverty and obedience. On washing days she so managed that the delicate Sisters did the household work, while the stronger washed; often taking for her share the cleaning of the boarders' refectory, and the washing of their dishes. At other times she undertook the cooking, and always arranged so as herself to set the example of that which she required in others, and invariably assisted as far as she was able in each variety of manual work, whether it was cutting furze out in the plantation, making repairs in the house, or decorating their chapel. On the occasion of sending the Sisters to

Roseau she said: 'Now, more than ever, we must remember our vow of Poverty. Those who are so happy as to go will feel its effects, we might call them the favourites of the Sacred Heart of Jesus, but you must first try your strength, and understand that it is only by denying ourselves, and practising strict economy, that we shall be able to extend our work to other fields of labour.' We have already had examples of the care with which she led her daughters at La Delivrande to cut off every little indulgence or superfluity, in order to help out the struggling foundation of Norwood, and bring down a greater blessing from God on their own house.

With regard to the second vow in religion, she was most faithful and watchful in the mortification of her senses, and, having once caught herself looking out vacantly on the road during recreation, she humbly begged her Admonitress to tell her at once if she observed her cast a glance beyond the enclosure. Obedience was the leading mark of Mother St. Mary's holiness. The whole history of her noviceship, as well as of each foundation, or new work undertaken by her, impresses clearly and deeply this character on her spiritual life. We may add that she was in the hands of her Superiors like the servant in the Gospel, doing or leaving things undone according to the word of command. When a friend wished her to go to London to consult a more experienced doctor, she replied that she would only do so if the Bishop ordered her, because her principle was to follow exclusively the prescriptions of the medical man of the house. Her friend then said she would herself obtain the permission from the Bishop, but the good Mother promptly answered that she hoped the Bishop had sufficient consideration for her religious profession not to order to do anything against the spirit of the rule.

During the long period of six years in which Father Saulet placed her under obedience to one of the lay-sisters she was constantly called upon to act against her own judgement and opinions, yet she did this most patiently and faithfully. She was even obliged to ask the Sister's permission to have the least things which she required, and was freely censured by her, being more than once brought, through her fault, under a severe reprimand. Yet the humble Mother never spoke of this, and not one of the Sisters who knew her most intimately ever discovered, until after her death, under how rigid a censorship her administration had been placed. She bore without a murmur the blame of measures which she herself had disapproved of in her heart, and thus united the truest humility to her perfect obedience. This spirit naturally fostered in Mother St. Mary the love of order and punctuality, the strict observance of which she combined with that gay and ever-ready compliance which springs from the full obedience of the heart. Her talent for administration and for the division and distribution of work was remarkable, and left no margin for wasted moments.

During a time when the community at La Delivrande was much tried by sickness, she wrote: 'How does regularity fare in the midst of all your sickness? Remember it is the duty of Superiors to preserve this unrelaxed. I am afraid some may find specious pretexts for loosening the strings, whereas I would say; *Everything must give way to regularity.* I beg of you to attend to this point from morning till night. God will bless you if order and punctuality flourish.' In writing to a religious she says: 'Bear the rule in mind, love it, foster it, practise it, my dearest child, let it be your daily bread. Look at it as the helmsman watches the compass, that he may steer his ship aright. We are sure in following it not to be shipwrecked in our course towards eternity. Regularity deals a deadly blow against all independence, our actions only pass current with God when they bear the stamp of obedience.

'Wherever you are, each day, on rising, in your meditations and examens, make a firm resolution to begin anew the complete observance of the rule. When nature craves to resume its rights, *Sursum corda.* Each precept of the rule is a separate step of the ladder that reaches to Jesus. To neglect the rule through inadvertence is an imperfection; we should fear to scandalize the younger Sisters by it. It is not necessary to be in the chapel in order to meditate, we must be able to say, like the Spouse in the Canticle: "I sleep, but my heart watches," that is, my heart prays to Jesus, loves Jesus. A good religious should be able to say: "While I am at the recreation, my heart thinks of Jesus; while I work for the children, I do this in union with Jesus. Meditation is the last duty from which we should dispense ourselves. Each action offered to God, and done in union with Him, is a continual meditation; but without this interior spirit we run the risk of losing all benefit to ourselves while we are busy working for others. In your examens see if you have considered things as God views them, or if you have followed the impulses of your passions. The tendency of your heart towards God must not be a strain which fatigues the mind, but a loving waiting upon Him by faith. Consider Jesus as always by your side and present with you. There is unknown sweetness in that thought, and it is a constant incentive to you. Rejoice in making sacrifices for Him.'

Thus did Mother St. Mary lead up souls along the path of recollection and mortification to a spirit of tender piety and devotion. She taught her religious to study the life of Jesus, and afterwards to say: 'Jesus meek and humble of Heart, make my heart like unto Thine.' If we forget our own interests to serve Jesus we shall do wonders, yet we must not be discouraged if we do not attain grand results. Let us in the purity of our motives seek only God's glory, worshipping Him by faith and love.' The Reverend Mother had a wonderful confidence in our Blessed Lady. From the origin of the Institute, the Blessed Virgin was solemnly chosen as chief Superior, and after each election the new Superior General laid the keys of the Convent at her feet, and pronounced an act of consecration recognizing her as sovereign mistress. All her feasts were celebrated with peculiar devotion. During the month of May the good Mother endeavoured to communicate her own sentiments of tender piety and filial confidence to the hearts of both religious and pupils. The Sisters came every evening to burn the list of their practices with incense at the feet of the Faithful Virgin; the children, after a day in which they had not been found fault with, were privileged to offer a flower, and tapers were given in reward of certain good points.

The ejaculation, 'Sweet Heart of Mary, be my salvation,' was familiar to Mother St. Marie, and she composed, in honour of Mary's Fidelity, the following prayer, which will always be doubly dear to her children: 'O Faithful Virgin, be thou blessed on account of thy Fidelity. Through thee all good has come to us. What can we render thee for so many graces? We offer thee the fidelity of our hearts. Thou hast ever been faithful to us; be still to us a Faithful Mother; we will be faithful to thee; obtain for us the grace to be ever faithful to thy Divine Son. Amen.[1]

If the Faithful Virgin is in a special way the Mother of the orphan, we may say with truth that she obtained for Mother St. Mary a wonderfully large hearted charity and affection towards them. She spoke from her heart in these words: 'I do so love those religious who understand our children, who understand their own vow and what it imposes on them, and who seek to live for the orphans. Those who wish me to love them specially have but to do this. Be, then, everything to these children, and God's eye will rest on you with complacency. If you dislike being employed among the children, listen to the teaching of faith, and your dislike will at once be overcome. It seems to me that the greatest reward of a religious of the Faithful Virgin should be to be employed in the care of them. Will the happy day ever come for me when, relieved of every other charge, I shall be named Mistress of the Orphans in either house? Religious should ask nothing and refuse nothing, but I permit them to long for this beloved charge. All perfection for us may be summed up in three things: God's will, God's glory, and the salvation of souls. The accomplishment of the work he has confided to us should be the moving power of all our thoughts, desires, and actions. Our whole life should have reference to the salvation of our children. There is not a single quarter of an hour in our existence wherein we were dispensed from the obligation of accomplishing this vow. There is no business so important for us. The children's good is the chief consideration. The best way of proving our love of God is to hinder a sin. If our vow doubles the merit of our actions it also doubles our obligations. If our devotedness shortens our life our crown will be all the brighter, and you will but enter the sooner into the joy of your Lord.'

Mother St. Mary dwelt carefully on the general motives and the principles in detail which must influence and guide the carrying out of this vow. 'See that you yourself are humble in success; take care not to be vain when the children do well, but attribute all to God who blesses your efforts. If

[1] In the diocese of Southwark an indulgence of forty days ' is granted for the recitation of this prayer.

you rob God of His glory He will be jealous. He will withdraw the grace that gives you success, and leave you to your own devices, when failure will convince you how little you can do by yourself. You must be happy in being employed with our children. Beware of the petty feelings of jealousy which would lead one to wish to be exclusively with the children, or to be preferred by them to others. Accustom yourselves to suffer, in order to obtain grace for yourselves and for your children. This suffering will come both from them and from yourselves, and will make you always practise virtue in some way or other for their sake. To succeed in training children you must strive to be self-possessed at all times, to be even in temper, and equitable in dealing justly with all. Virtue must be rather insinuated by example than daily enforced by punishment or constant admonition. If you manage them with tact, and persuade them to wish to improve, you will have enabled them to gain something, and will yourself be able to say, "My children have improved, they have behaved better than yesterday." Lead your children to love God, let them learn from your example to sacrifice pleasure to duty; inspire them with a strict sense of integrity and of delicacy of thought and action, showing your pleasure in observing these in them during their games, &c.

'If a child resists you, pray for her, pleading the merits of the blood of Jesus on her behalf. I have never found that fail me. Walk in God's presence, invoke your guardian angel as well as that of the child; say with all simplicity, "My good angel, lead that child's heart to accept what I ask of her."

'Be yourself also the guardian angel of each, removing from her path whatever may do her harm.

'Inspire the children with sentiments of filial duty; make them feel that, if they have good will, a thread may guide them. Above all, study each one's character. You will find that succeed admirably with one which wholly fails with another; while tone, manner, circumstances, all must be taken into account. You will make many mistakes before attaining what you desire to effect, only persevere, and pray to God to guide you. You must not decide that a certain plan is bad because you personally have not succeeded in its application, since another may find it works excellently with her; be assured that by prayer and perseverance you too will discover the right means. Let the children feel satisfied that what they do right will be acknowledged, and that you will sometimes for certain good reasons shut your eyes to little faults. Let failure never bring discouragement in you; energetically set to work to find out the cause of it, and begin over again. Have as much patience with yourself as with the children. We require to excite the emulation of young people, being careful never to damp their ardour; when they have repaired a fault at once, raise them in their own eyes, and in feelings of self-respect.

While a mistress is employed with children she must be exact in fulfilling her religious duties, anxious and ingenious to combine them with her other work. I should like to see her during class time so lovingly realize our Lord's presence as to turn readily to Him in each difficulty and consult Him what to do. Look out for and make immediate use of each favourable moment for making an impression on the hearts of the children, especially of those who are unamiable, passionate, or stubborn. Make much of even their weak efforts for the sake of encouraging them, and of producing stronger good desires. Prove to them, and try to get them to see that without order and tidiness they will never be successful or happy in after-life.'

It was a great consolation to Mother St. Mary to hear that the Assistant had, on visiting La Delivrande, found every custom and regulation as faithfully and exactly observed as it had been six years before. This spirit, she remarked, could alone secure the primitive zeal and success of a religious foundation.

Chapter XXI

Letters of Mother St. Mary.

The following letters are given, not as containing any incidents of interest or spiritual instructions of a strongly marked or original character, but simply because they show the tenderness of affection which united Mother St. Mary to her spiritual daughters and to the children. The gentleness and firmness of the hand which she held over them, and the sacredness in her eyes of that distinct work to which God called her and her religious congregation, namely, the care of orphans, may be easily read in every line.

I

'My dear child, —When I referred to "my being silent, notwithstanding your sorrow," I meant to suggest that you should go before the Blessed Sacrament, and that there you would find true light, and strength, and courage. Abandon all then, and you will find all. Accustom yourself to make our Lord your friend, your confidant, your refuge. He can never fail you, even after your acts of folly or of over-haste; tell them all to Him, and calmly beg of Him to help you to repair them, and to prevent their doing harm to our dear children. But be not surprised at falling into them.

'Let there be no anxious looking forward to future days of trial that we may never see. Pass today well, tomorrow will bring its own grace with it.'

II

'Oh, yes; what is impossible to man is possible to God, my little child! He will not fail you if you turn to Him with faith and confidence. Temptation is not sin; our Lord said to St. Paul it was good for him to be tempted. Above all, do not allow yourself to be discouraged. Remember I will not have you sad, nor wrapped up in your own sorrows, that would be the greatest snare the devil could lay for you. You would grieve the good God and your Mother that loves you.'

III

'... Courage, courage, dear child! Trample down nature with both feet at once! Ever raise your eyes to Heaven in difficult moments. ...Yes, more than ever I forbid you to be discouraged. A missionary alone in China, without a guide, or spiritual help, or advice, or a mother to love her, has more to suffer than my little English missionary, although I do acknowledge she has something to offer her Spouse. But you know you must become a saint, and one of my greatest joys in Heaven will be to see you follow the Lamb in His Glory. Then we shall think no more of the privations and sufferings of today. I think of you often, I pray for you, and love you, my child; pray for me. *Sursum corda,* dear child. Yes, love Jesus with all the energy of a heart made to love the only object worthy of love. Remain in His Heart during my absence, lifting up your own so high, so very high, that the devil cannot get at it, but sees from a distance that it is fixed on Jesus! Yes, Jesus intends to have you all for Himself, and men are merely the help that conduct you to Him. He is jealous of your whole heart, that is why He separates you from me at certain times. He wants to reign alone in your heart; do you not often hear Him say: "Give Me this heart, My child –it is Mine?"'

IV

'Take courage, my child; it is in suffering and difficulties overcome for God that we show Him our love. Measure your love by His; see how He separated Himself from His Mother on earth that He might prove this love for you. See how He has suffered in every way for us. Go to the Garden of Olives, to Mount Calvary, to the Cross, you will find Him there, and me too, in a little corner, showing Him to you, and asking you if you have suffered that sweat of blood, or the agony afterwards from which He rises exhausted to go and suffer the torments of His Passion. Never may there be any discouragement or melancholy, but the cross carried with love, even when we cry: *My father, my Father, why hast Thou forsaken me?* Is there negligence in your duties because you suffer? Oh, what cowardice!

'It is then that we should redouble our vigilance, because we feel nature craves to turn aside, and we ought to be afraid to listen to its murmurings. Let us live for God Who will unite us to Himself for all eternity, provided we have denied ourselves for Him on earth. I bless you on condition that you will be what my heart wishes you to be.'

V

'How happy I am to have given you pleasure! Be simple, like the divine Child, Who had but one thought... to do His Father's will! Yes, He does permit you to love your Superiors, and your Superiors also to love you. I, too, am the first to put this into practice. I promise to say a little word, and a long one too to God for you. I know how good you all are: that does good to my heart.

'Pray for me.'

VI

'A little word from me will make you happy, dear child; why refuse it? It makes one so happy to give pleasure, and it is so hard, on the contrary, to inflict pain. Be, then, always good, kind, gentle, devoted to your Mother, your Sisters, and your children; be fervent, and get me on my feet again, if that be God's will. I send you a very earnest maternal blessing.'

VII

'Rest courageously on our Saviour's Heart with St. John: you will only be able to go thither when you are good, or wish to become so. And as you cannot be weaned all of a sudden from what nourishes human affection, rest also in the heart of a Mother who loves you, and wishes to see you a saint at any price. Adieu –all for God.'

VIII

'Dear child, you will soon be able to write to me and say, "God is well pleased. I have overcome my weariness of mind, my sadness; I have devoted myself entirely to my duties; I live on duty; God blesses it, and all goes well." I do not mean that this will cost you nothing. Oh, no. I am aware how hard it is to put oneself on one side, and go on in spite of the revolt of nature. I know it is hard not to fall under the Cross when it is heavy, to say *Sursum corda*, to seem strong when you feel weak, to support and fortify others without giving way yourself. Yet that is what a good religious should do –what you must do with the children that God has confided to you. He counts on you, and so do I. Are you going to disappoint us and become a spiritless woman, without energy and without faith? But you have faith, and I appeal to it, and to your heart, to rise immediately on reading this letter. My child, YOU MUST. *Obey your Mother*. Rise, go to the chapel, and pass from it another person –a valiant woman, a daughter according to my heart. I bless you. Your Mother more in heart than in name.'

IX

'I send you my good angel to whisper in your ear what I would say myself. Oh, dear child, listen to the voice of faith, be a religious of faith, be supernatural. Ask your own good angel what I would permit, what I would say, for God's glory and the children's good, and the salvation of your own soul.

'You know that God and I desire the same thing for you. If I thus refer to myself, it is because you know very well what I think in the matter.'

X

To two Sisters on their profession

'My dear children, —My heart longs to tell you how very much I rejoice at your happiness, which I fully enter into and share. In spirit I will follow you to the altar on this great day, as I joyfully gave my vote for you. The only sacrifice is that I cannot see you with my own eyes, but God so wills it. This is our motto on earth. When He reunites us we will bless Him; when He separates us we shall bless Him again.

'Be good religious, love the Cross, learn to carry it daily, and I answer for your happiness in his world and the next. Tell the dear novices how tenderly I love them, and appropriate your own portion. Make this oblation of yourself in behalf of your poor Mother, who is in such need of help from all her daughters.'

XI

'Dear child, let us live by faith, and aspire after the next world. Above all, do not ask to live without suffering. Let us try to suffer truly with Jesus, and for Jesus. Suffering is the money of the religious, with which she purchases souls and virtues, and Heaven for herself and others. Then be rich to win souls; buy for me, I will buy for you, and will carry you in my maternal heart.'

XII

'My poor little child, —Yes, I like the letters that you write with such simplicity and confidence. I read your soul in them, and that is what I want. Write in this way, but do not reason so much on your state, nor take too close an account of it. Go on with your eyes shut, by the path which is shown you, and I promise you I will not let go of you... All the better that you are not spared; your nature will be all the sooner overcome; it is because you are loved that you are treated so. It is true I spoil you, but my little child needs an old grandmother to give her sugar and sweetmeats to encourage her. It is not that I love you less than the other little ones, but because the bow cannot always be bent without losing its spring, my part is the sweetest, and my heart rejoices in it, for you are dear to me.

'I am glad you have got over ... that fault. Now you must work to overcome ... this other one, which can be done with God's grace, and this I earnestly beg for you. You know I like to give you pleasure, but it is not always in my power.'

A Sister having made some difficulty about going to the common work, she wrote:

XIII

'Dear child, —The *interests of Jesus* suffer in the common work, because there are not Sisters enough. *He* had counted on you, and I also... Come! Can you give Him nothing in your day? Tell me simply what you can do for Him by putting yourself to a slight inconvenience. I leave it to you: sometimes one can put off for another day. The great retreat for which your assistant is taken from you, is also for *Him* –is it not? I expect your reply.'

This Sister, won over by such gentleness of reproof, returned to her obedience, and received the following commendation:

'My child, your note consoles me, and I send you with both hands the blessing of Jesus, Who is pleased with you. Yes, Mary, His good Mother, will help you tomorrow, and bless you today by the hand of her who holds her place, and who is gratified by your docility.'

XIV

To a religious on the death of her father

'My poor child, —I have just received the letter announcing to me the death of your father. Whose heart better than mine can understand your grief? Oh, my daughter, lift up your heart in faith, and let us do all we can that he may speedily reach the bliss of Heaven. In the hour and half which has elapsed since I received your letter, I have done all I could for that dear soul. Father Vesque prays with me, and sympathizes in your grief. I could not read your letter to him without tears. We are both orphans now. One must pass through that trial to know all the heart-breaking and loss of protection and affection constantly occurring on earth. In a few days I shall see you, and embrace you with a mother's love... . There are visitors here: I have left them a moment to tell you that on the other side of the sea there is a heart that feels for you and with you, and prays for you and for him whom you so justly regret, for he was universally respected and esteemed.

'May Jesus and His holy Mother console you, strengthen you, and be all in all to you, my very dear child.'

XV

To a novice

'First of all I send you, according to your wish, a *big* blessing, a blessing of strength and generosity to overcome yourself. How pleased I am to see that you try so much to get the better of your nature, which, without that, would be a despotic tyrant, unless you manage to conquer it while young. We may have no peace nor truce with our failings, but wage continual war, even if we had to sweat blood like our Divine Master. Too covetous is he to whom God is not all sufficient, dear child. Yet your poor heart sets itself upon creatures, and is not contented with the Creator; it seeks right and left for human consolations. Believe me, if you found any in this Mother, she would no longer be of any use to you. You must have a Mother that loves you, and she does, be assured, and I too, since you desire to hear this. I can say it truly with all my heart, but I love you *far better* when I find you a child *of faith*, who seeks above all to please God and overcome her passions. Without discouragement often turn to God, to the Faithful Virgin, and understand, the more you wish me to love you, the more *holy* you must become; and thereupon I bless you.'

XVI

'My very dear child, —Your letter has much consoled me. God will do His work in you. You will be a good religious, though it will cost you much, but acquired virtue is more solid than natural virtue.

'Your disposition is not good, but grace is stronger, and at any price it must triumph in you. Bless God with me to have put you into the hands of one who will allow nature no quarter, it is the greatest proof of her love. For myself I do not refuse a little sugar-plum to my spoilt child from time to time, to help her to get on, but I had rather send her a blessing of faith to follow the advice given her. I agree fully with you, and enter into your views of what you must do to become a good religious, and I add, *child, be faithful* –be a victim of humility, of mortification, a victim for Heaven, a victim for life, happy in eternity. For that I send you the blessing pronounced on obedience, on courage, and you will become my submissive and charitable daughter, model first of the novitiate, and afterwards of the community, and so you will be the happiness of all who love you, of whom I am one.'

XVII

'My dear child, —Come and work in England, for there too God will put up with our defects, provided we try to correct ourselves and live for Him alone –He has cast a look on you and chosen you to work for Him. Take to yourself then a missionary's heart and courage; come and devote yourself for the souls of these little ones who expect you, and will love you as another mother whom God sends them.

'Offer to God all the sacrifices your heart makes on leaving La

Delivrande, from which you are not, on that account, separated. Obedience calls you; come at its call, my child, your heart raised high and generously disposed. On Saturday I shall receive you with open arms, happy to install and acclimatize you, before I return to France. Adieu, I bless you with the blessing of strength, zeal, and charity, and shall be happy in seeing you soon.'

XVIII

'Be not too much afraid of a cross only looming in the future, we have not yet received grace for anticipated crosses — "Sufficient unto the day is the evil thereof;" and perhaps what we tremble at as a misfortune may turn out a great happiness, when we come to see it clearly in eternity –so little fascinates us here below, and deceives us in persons and things. What we want is a simple straightforward heart, seeking conformity with God, and sure that then all will be well –leaving our future along with our sufferings in His hands, which will be only what He permits and sends us under one shape or other, from one person or another. Let us receive all as from Him, and bow our heads before Him in adoration, full of confidence that He will never fail us, and will then especially be all in all to us when He withdraws help, support, and consolation.

'It is very hard, my child, to feel as though all were failing you, even the earth on which you stand, and to see nothing but chaos in the future. If we look at things in the mass we are disconcerted, but if trusting in God we address ourselves to each thing in its turn doing the best we can, then all will come right, and we shall see that a powerful hand has helped and supported us.'

Chapter XXII

Present state of Mother St. Mary's work.

There is an intimate and permanent union between a religious congregation and its founder. The spirit and work of the congregation still continue to emanate from and represent to us the peculiar vocation of its founder, while he still lives before us in the life and good works of his spiritual children. It is therefore fair that we should not conclude this biography of Mother St. Mary without a short sketch of the progress of her foundations since her death.

At La Delivrande the orphanage contains one hundred and twenty orphans, by far the majority of whom are entirely supported by the house. The boarding-school is flourishing, and the novitiate carefully preserves and venerates the traditions of their first Mother.

As her death approached, two ideas much occupied her mind, which Dr. Vesque agreed with her in thinking very desirable and which she herself hoped to see realized. The first of these was the establishment of uncloistered Sisters, who, while entering the congregation on the same footing as the other religious, would not be subjected to the same strictness of enclosure, and could thus, under the authority of the local Superior, visit the orphans in different situations, in order to encourage and advise them, and attend to them in sickness or in any other circumstances which specially called for their assistance; they could also accompany the children in their walks, excursions, and the like.

All this has been since effected, and the good already resulting from it proves that the Foundress had been guided by the Spirit of God in seeking thus to develop her congregation.

Mother St. Mary's second long cherished desire was to establish a home for former members of the orphanage. She had often regretted not being able to receive again for a time children who had been educated in the house, but it was not till 1861 that an opportunity was afforded of beginning that part of the good Mother's design.

The girls are now placed out soon as they are capable of filling the situation chosen for them. But the house which they leave still maintains intercourse with them, by correspondence, annual circulars, meetings on Sunday for those in the neighbourhood, by an annual retreat which all may attend, by the distribution of prizes to those who have good certificates from their mistress and employers, and by occasional visits; for all these means are used to encourage perseverance amongst the children who have left. Moreover all orphans who for any reason, except misconduct, lose their situation are allowed to return to the house which has brought them up, or to whichever house may be nearest them, where they can be secure from harm till another position is found for them. When ill they can also return to find the care necessary for their recovery, or to be prepared for a happy and holy death. The inmates of the 'Home' are kept apart from those belonging to the orphanage.

Although Mother St. Mary had been frequently urged to give a distinct and permanent shape to the constitutions of the Institute of which she was Foundress, she had thought it better to delay until the nature and extent of the undertaking, which she and her congregation were destined to accomplish, had more fully declared themselves, and until she had acquired greater experience in the external working of the orphanage. The foundation, however, of a Mission Convent in the West Indies, rendered the drawing up of fixed constitutions a more urgent matter, and the Reverend Mother collected some notes which had been the fruits of earnest meditation before God, and submitted them for revision to the Bishop of Roseau. Very shortly afterwards God removed both these by death, and the papers which possessed such value were, with some few expectations, destroyed. Fortunately she had so often declared her mind upon the most important points and had to such an extent embodied them in her personal rule at La Delivrande, and still more at Norwood, that, when all had been drawn out on paper by Reverend Mother General, under the help and well-informed direction of the late Bishop of Southwark, a copious set of notes was found to be the result. These were placed in the hands of a holy and experienced religious for due arrangement and expression, and the constitutions and rules thus framed were taken to Rome by the Superior General in 1870 and presented before the Holy Father, who granted to them the first approbation of the Holy See, and added the kindest words of encouragement on the undertaking.

The Institute at this moment comprises eight different houses. Those of Folkestone and Lulworth, in the diocese of Plymouth, are dependent on Norwood. In France, besides the Mother-house of La Delivrande, the Institute is beginning a foundation in Paris; and two rich and generous ladies, the Marchioness de Songueil, who has a grandchild in the Congregation of the Faithful Virgin, and the Countess de Coislin, cousin of Mother St. Mary, have founded the two houses of Pigeon, near Mortagne, in the department of Orne, dating from the year 1868, and of Moulins, in the department of Alliers, begun in 1870. Besides these the foundation at Roseau must be counted in the list. The Holy Father has authorized the Convent at Norwood to open a novitiate, thus enabling English subjects to make their profession in this country.

As more definite interest attaches in England to the progress of the house at Norwood, we give a fuller account of it. The community had not long to wait for sensible proofs of their Mother's protection and intercession in Heaven. As we have already mentioned, a very short time after her death they were able to get possession of a piece of ground close by, which they had before made many fruitless attempts to obtain, and which was not likely ever to come in to their hands. In 1861 and 1862 two generous benefactors, Mr. Whiteside and Mr. Pagliano, left to the Institute by will sums which when combined amounted to nearly £3,000. This helped to build a new wing, and the increased accommodation enabled the nuns to receive from the workhouses Catholic children, whom the law authorized to be placed in certain specified schools of their own religion. After undergoing an inspection from the Poor Law Board, they obtained the necessary authorization, and this was the earliest instance of such permission being granted to a Catholic school. What gave the fact more importance in the eyes of the community was that it occurred on the 20th of January, a day especially marked in the annals of the Congregation as the anniversary of the miraculous cure of its Foundress, in 1835; and as the day on which they celebrate their feast of the Faithful Virgin.

Of late the number of orphans admitted has increased rapidly until the full complement of three hundred and thirty has been attained, and so many expenses have been incurred in extending the precincts of the orphanage, that up to the present moment the large community of Sisters is still left wholly without proper accommodation, each gift of charity presented having, with great self-denial and generosity, been devoted to the immediate advantage of those under their charge. Even in 1868 the large rooms serving as a provisionary chapel had long become inadequate to receive the crowds attending Mass and Benediction; and at the last confirmation held by Dr. Grant, his Lordship dwelt much on the urgency of the case and on the necessity of promptly carrying out the proposed plans for building a more becoming sanctuary. The necessary funds were however not forthcoming ; and from Rome, whither he had gone to attend the Vatican Council, Dr. Grant sent to the Mother Superior a special blessing on all those who would help to build a church in honour of the Faithful Virgin.

About the very same time the committee charged with receiving the subscriptions of the Catholic public for the erection of a monument to the memory of Mr. Charles Langdale, very kindly gave a surplus sum to the orphanage at Norwood; but as this was not sufficient for the erection of a special building, it was decided that the temporary chapel should be converted into a classroom for a hundred more children, and that the funds of the Langdale memorial should be employed in erecting a building which was to abut on the future church. After the death of Dr. Grant, June 1, 1870, the Vicar General, now Bishop of Southwark, and the Chapter of St. George's Cathedral, begged that the church at Norwood might be erected to the memory of the holy Bishop, who had himself chosen it for his last resting place. This pious thought met with general approbation, and in the month of July following the first stone was laid with all solemnity by Lord Howard of Glossop and His Grace the Duke of Norfolk, surrounded by many of the clergy and nobility. A subscription list was opened and the work was so actively pushed forward, that on the first day of the following June, 1871, the anniversary of Dr. Grant's death, the church was opened by the Archbishop of Westminster, the Bishop of Southwark, and Dr. Morris, Bishop of Troy. Six moths later a transept was completed and blessed by the Bishop, and the Catholic congregation of Norwood was enabled to attend the services of the Church in a building entirely separated from the community.

In 1870 Dr. Grant, during a visit to Rome, obtained from the Holy Father a special blessing for the Norwood community, and a plenary indulgence for all who should visit the church on the 14th of September, being the twenty-fifth anniversary of the arrival of the religious of the Faithful Virgin in England. Some zealous benefactors present on that occasion proposed to form a jubilee fund, in the hope of thus collecting the sum necessary for building the cells and other community rooms, the want of which was more felt in proportion as the number of the Sisters increased. But the time proved unfavourable, because Catholic charity was engaged on all sides in new works and new schools. After the lapse of five years a sum amounting to £ 5,000 has been subscribed, a large part of which was given by one charitable benefactor. In consequence however of the high price now paid for labour and material, the Convent is £2,000 short of the present contract. Besides this the building of the cloisters and sacristy is perforce postponed to some future day. They have therefore made a new appeal, and they cherish the hope that pious persons, who read the life of their Foundress, will desire to place some stones in the walls of a future Convent, and to inscribe their names among those of the benefactors of the orphans.

CONTENTS

Deo Gratias
March 2012
Proof Reader: Lawrence Farrugia
Typist, spell checker and designer: Sister Rosalía Pastor